Sexual Misconduct in the Schoolhouse

Sexual Misconduct in the Schoolhouse

Prevention Strategies for Principals, Teachers, Coaches, and Students

Second Edition

William L. Fibkins

ROWMAN & LITTLEFIELD
Lanham • Boulder • New York • London

Published by Rowman & Littlefield
A wholly owned subsidiary of The Rowman & Littlefield Publishing Group, Inc.
4501 Forbes Boulevard, Suite 200, Lanham, Maryland 20706
www.rowman.com

Unit A, Whitacre Mews, 26-34 Stannary Street, London SE11 4AB

Copyright © 2017 by William L. Fibkins

All rights reserved. No part of this book may be reproduced in any form or by any electronic or mechanical means, including information storage and retrieval systems, without written permission from the publisher, except by a reviewer who may quote passages in a review.

British Library Cataloguing in Publication Information Available

Library of Congress Cataloging-in-Publication Data Available

ISBN: 978-1-4758-2199-4 (cloth : alk. paper)
ISBN: 978-1-4758-2200-7 (pbk. : alk. paper)
ISBN: 978-1-4758-2201-4 (electronic)

Dedication

This book is dedicated to Dr. Alan Goldberg and Dr. Richard Pearson, now retired professors in the counseling education program at Syracuse University. Al and Dick were my mentors at Syracuse and taught me the important lesson that professionals involved in close relationships with students need to know how to set clear boundaries, keep their own personal needs in good order, and have a support system available if and when they find themselves becoming too personally involved in a student's life. As this book documents, there are real hazards and risks in guiding and advising needy, vulnerable adolescents. Al and Dick served their graduate students well by opening up the issue for discussion and offering ways to train and prepare teachers, coaches, counselors, and administrators to avoid taking on friendship, surrogate parent, and savior roles that can lead to sexual misconduct.

Needy students are best served by caregivers who are well trained and aware that they, like their needy students, can be at risk, given disruptions, losses, and setbacks in their own personal lives. Best to prepare professionals by raising their awareness rather than making the dangerous assumption that sexual misconduct only happens to professionals in other schools. I believe that awareness can help stem the tide of sexual misconduct and promote open discussions in our schools rather than, as is the case now, being seen as a taboo subject and a problem "that can't happen here." I thank Al and Dick for that gift of knowing.

Contents

Preface ix

Introduction xiii

I: A Guide to Preventing Sexual Misconduct by Teachers and Coaches as Seen in 2006   1

1   Issues in Facing and Solving the Problem of Sexual Misconduct   3
2   Cases of Teachers Who Became Involved in Sexual Misconduct   29
3   Cases of Coaches Who Become Involved in Sexual Misconduct   41
4   Cases of Predator Teachers   67
5   Training Teachers, Coaches, and Students to Avoid Sexual Misconduct   81

II: Since 2006 Many Schools Have Abandoned Their Mission to Protect Students   113

6   A Perfect Storm Brings a New Wave of Sexual Misconduct to the Schools   115
7   The Tragic Stories of the Lives of Students and Educators Involved in Sexual Misconduct Are Being Hidden behind a Wall of Cold, Impersonal Data   119
8   A Case Study of What Administrators Should Not Do When a Potential Sexual Misconduct Issue Emerges   125
9   A Case Study of What an Administrator Should Do When a Potential Sexual Misconduct Issue Emerges   133
10   Criteria for How the Building Principal Can Build an Effective School Policy to Help Prevent Sexual Misconduct   143

Conclusion 147
References 153

Preface

There is a need for a second edition of the book *Innocence Denied: A Guide to Preventing Sexual Misconduct by Teachers and Coaches*, which was published in 2006. That first edition, which comprises part I of this "how to" book, was an effort to lay the groundwork for the need for schools to develop programs to prevent the growing problem of sexual misconduct in the schools.

For example, the book provided a detailed example of training programs for untrained educators to help them avoid sexual misconduct that can arise in one-on-one contact with at-risk students, a rising problem as more and more students were coming into secondary schools with emotional, academic, health, and well-being problems and at risk of seeking liaisons with educators who appear to be caring adult figures but who themselves were at risk to such behavior. This is a combustible mix, particularly in light of the fact that many schools lacked adequate training and counseling interventions needed to head off at-risk students and educators from entering into relations that would end up ruining their lives.

But a lot has happened since the first edition was published, leaving many secondary schools and their staff overwhelmed and dispirited. An unparalleled assault on the schools by outside education reformers has arrived at the national and state levels and unleashed a powerful campaign to raise standards, test scores, and achievement levels.

Since 2006, this assault on the schools has created a culture in which many parents and students are raising the questions, "Does anyone care about us? Is anyone listening to our needs and problems? Is anyone watching over us?" Good questions. As this second edition suggests, the stultifying arrival of reform has turned our schools into factories where educators are being forced into new roles as piece workers trying to glue all the complicated aspects of reform into a winning picture.

The roles of building principals, counselors, and teachers have changed. They now march to a different drum as soldiers in the Reform Wars. Their work now is all about making sure that they are on the same page as reformers, making sure their mandates are being implemented, that test scores are rising, and that everyone is marching to the same tune, "God Sent Us Reformers to Make Our Schools Better." For any educator, this is a blues song with no happy ending.

As a result, a perfect storm has encircled our schools and staff, forcing caring building principals, guidance counselors, and teachers to abandon their helping and intervention role with at-risk students in order to feed the never-ending demands of reformers to do more and do better. The corporate world with its ongoing demands to sell its product has arrived in the public schools in the guise of reform and as a result has forced educators to give up a role that was the reason why many building principals, counselors, and teachers went into education: to help students with their personal and well-being problems and be all they can be.

They have become servants to powerful reform interests and been forced to abandon their dream of simply being in the good company of students, teaching, counseling, and guiding them as they navigate through the problems of teenage life. What we have in many schools are educators who are too busy to care and watch over and protect vulnerable and naïve teens.

Isolation and anonymity have become the norm and building principals, counselors, and teachers are closing their doors and focusing on surviving the paper crush that comes with reform. While reform is described as making things better by removing faults and defects, putting a stop to abuses and malpractices, and introducing better procedures, what we have in many schools is reform that seems to increase the faults and lack of responsibility of educators and the personal and emotional defects of students.

Students are savvy. They know when the doors of help are closed. They know when they arrive at the point at which no one is listening and all the once-open doors for help are boarded up. That's the moment when vulnerable students often find themselves involved in risky behavior, mischief, trouble, and big problems because there is no experienced mentor and adviser around when they walk the hallways after school looking for someone to care for them.

And desperation to connect with their school, teachers, and peers often leads students into problematic relations with at-risk educators. Usually it's an educator who is going through a separation or divorce, has home, work, and emotional problems, and has had no training in how to handle close one-on-one contact with students.

It's a combustible mix that finds fertile ground and increases sexual misconduct in schools where the adult protectors such as building principals, counselors, and teachers are too busy reforming, not taking notice of the students they are responsible for caring for and protecting, or looking the other way and not intervening because they feel "it's not my job" or "I am too busy to get involved."

As this second edition points out, the formula to increased sexual misconduct is simple: at-risk educator, lack of training for the educator in how to handle one-on-one relationships with students, lack of close colleagues to turn to when the educator finds him or herself crossing professional boundaries, and lack of available counseling intervention for both the student and the educator.

And contrary to the public belief that the main culprit in sexual misconduct is educators who are perverts who prey on naïve and lonely students, it is my experience that most cases of sexual misconduct grow out of close contact between at-risk students and at-risk educators, not perverts.

Secondary schools are sensual places, starting with the clothing students wear, their language, interests, music, dancing, and partying. Hormones run high among students. Attractions, sexual activity, etcetera, are in. This is not one's 1950s school in which bodies were hidden with layers of clothes. And remember there is not much age difference between a seventeen-year-old student and a twenty-five-year-old teacher.

Sensuality is in the air in our secondary schools and holds a powerful place in the school's culture. Those in charge of protecting, caring for, and guiding our vulnerable and sensual teens need to be provided the necessary supervision, training, and, when necessary, counseling intervention and dismissal to make sure our students are protected.

As this book suggests, advocating that sexual misconduct can't happen in our schools and that no one on our staff would ever do such a thing is the talk of fools wearing blinders. Isn't it better to have educators trained to this reality rather than leave them vulnerable to emotions they may not be prepared to handle?

Becoming a master teacher requires more than being a master of academic material. It also means becoming a master of one's emotional self in order to deal successfully with the personal side of one's life as well as the students' personal lives. The opportunities for sexual misconduct have increased in our schools since 2006. It doesn't have to be this way.

The purpose of this second edition is to suggest that what we need to do is create many open doors for help in order to quickly respond to the cries of help by both at-risk students looking for someone to care for them and at-risk educators not seeing the red light of danger as they cross professional boundaries.

Lacking a variety of such interventions necessary to head off sexual misconduct, we must sadly conclude that the blame for the rise of sexual misconduct in the schools ultimately resides with those educators in leadership positions—school superintendents, building principals, counselors and school psychologist, and teacher leaders—who have abandoned their important roles to protect their students.

Yes, education reform has played a huge part in curtailing critical intervention services in the school, but educators in leadership positions in many schools have played a passive role by not fighting back to ensure that protection for at-risk students is not negotiable. It's time to stand up and for schools to reclaim their mandate to protect students and help them follow their dreams.

Introduction

This book is divided into two parts. Part I was published in 2006 and presented an overview of the problem of sexual misconduct and what schools can do to stop this abuse.

The goal of the book was to educate building principals, counselors, and teachers about sexual misconduct, provide a training model to better prepare school staff on how to avoid misconduct, encourage school leaders to upgrade their supervision efforts, and put in place support systems educators could turn to if they found themselves crossing professional boundaries with students. Here are the themes in the book:

- The issues involved in facing and solving the problem of sexual misconduct
- Cases of teachers who became involved in sexual misconduct
- Cases of coaches who became involved in sexual misconduct
- Case of predatory teachers
- Training teachers, coaches, and students to avoid sexual misconduct

This was a good beginning effort to help lift the curtain of denial about sexual misconduct and provide a wakeup call for school leaders to stop denying that sexual misconduct can't happen in their school and that educators are not at risk to such behavior.

However, the school world did not anticipate the magnitude of changes that swept through the schools soon after the publication of the first edition. Mandates for school reform, uniformed standards, and increased testing soon became the norm and within a short time became the public schools' number one priority.

As a result, many building principals, counselors, and teachers were forced to commit their energy and focus to reform issues while training, supervision, and intervention for educators on how to avoid sexual misconduct with students gathered little support and became a low priority in the new school world of education reform. Protecting and caring for students gave way to building principals, counselors, and teachers being forced to give 100 percent of their efforts to make reform succeed and test scores rise.

The need for a part II for this sexual misconduct book became clear as the perfect storm of school reform took its toll on educators, who found their roles being transformed from competent professionals with their own ideas to subservient roles carrying out the edicts of reform, politicians, and media gurus who had never spent a day in a classroom or visited their school.

And at the same time, many students found their young lives plagued with test after test, teachers weary keeping up with never-ending demands from reformers, and parents trying to figure out why their children were becoming physically and emotionally tired of all of the tests and clatter to improve.

However, in 2016 the tide appears to be changing and there is a growing effort to put a stop to the reforms that have been more about creating chaos than needed change in the schools. While it is true that reform efforts are highly funded, backed by powerful forces, and used to winning, more and more parents and educators are organizing to fight back against reform that they view as placing too much stress on their children as well as their teachers.

The major focus of this second edition, part II, is to aid this effort and remind parents and educators how much we have lost in protecting and caring for our students while being forced to embrace reforms developed by strangers to our schools.

Here are the themes in part II:

- A perfect storm brings a new wave of sexual misconduct into the schools
- The tragic stories of the lives of students and educators involved in sexual misconduct are being hidden behind a wall of cold, impersonal, statistics
- A case study of what administrators should not do when a potential case of sexual misconduct emerges
- A case study of what administrators should do when a potential sexual misconduct issue emerges
- Criteria for how the building principal can build an effective school policy to help prevent sexual misconduct

It is important for the reader to keep in mind that high school, junior high school, and middle school students exist in a world whose culture and values are vastly different from those of the community they live in.

Students may be housed in buildings very familiar to their parents, but once they enter the school house doors, they are in "their" world, a sexualized world that operates with its own rules and codes of behavior.

They might as well be educated in a spaceship traveling miles away that arrives each morning for pickup and delivers them back to the community in the afternoon. These schools are places where academics are supposed to reign, but the main draw for students in secondary school is learning how to navigate the sexual rejections and attractions of this "getting to be an adult in this risky world" time of their lives.

However, in many cases this is a lonely road many students have to navigate on their own. For example, when parents ask their children, "What did you do in school today?" they seldom get a truthful answer. Most teenagers play it safe and keep their real school life beyond the reach of inquiring, prying parents.

Mum's the word. Parents are no different. They are reluctant to reveal their own school acting out and misbehaviors from back in the day. They simply don't want "my boy or girl doing the things I did or dreamed of doing." Mum's the word for them as well and as a result it's a standoff, with usually no quarter given. Theirs is a dance with a mix of anger, stubbornness, and sometimes silent resistance to sharing the truth.

Yet many parents believe these are difficult times for teenagers and that it is harder to be a kid growing up in America today. They want their schools to be safe places and their children to be protected and cared for.

But there are students for whom change comes too suddenly. They end up testing the limits or not knowing what the limits are. They arrive from smaller elementary schools and find themselves in large schools, many with over two thousand students, which breed and encourage anonymity both for students and staff. They are literally thrown into these schools without real life experience and don't always understand the consequences that come with acting out behavior. They often find it hard to connect to their school, teachers, and peers and seek out an arena of safety and comfort. This can be true for at-risk students from every corner of student life: high achievers, marginal students, and star athletes.

It's important not to cast our secondary schools as peaceful kingdoms in which every student and staff member respect, care, and support each other. That's a fantasy land lived in by educators and parents who wish it to be true but have little sense of schools as they really are. Schools are not places where care, intimacy, and affection come easily for some students. Rejection is often the currency of choice in communicating.

As this second edition suggests, it is the job and responsibility of educators to know students and staff well who may be at risk to sexual misconduct, throw them a lifeline, and pull them back from the harm and disgrace coming their way. As this book suggests, a lifeline to help educators avoid sexual misconduct with students involves ongoing close supervision, training, observation, and intervention, required counseling, and loss of job when necessary.

This is the model of the world our children want and need for their care, protection, and security, a security many do not find at home or in the community. This book is about how educators can restore what has been abandoned for too long in the chase for reform. In the end, the blame for the increase in sexual misconduct in the schools ultimately resides with educators—administrators, counselors, teachers, and coaches—who have failed to care for and protect their students.

This book asks the question, "Isn't it better to have educators be well trained to avoid sexual misconduct before it is allowed to happen, take hold, and flourish?" And when at-risk students ask, "Is anyone listening, does anyone care?" there will hopefully be someone to answer.

I

A Guide to Preventing Sexual Misconduct by Teachers and Coaches as Seen in 2006

Chapter One

Issues in Facing and Solving the Problem of Sexual Misconduct

INTRODUCTION

This book makes the argument that there is no epidemic of teacher sexual misconduct in our schools. Nevertheless, too many teachers engage in such misconduct. As Edward Stancik, the former special commissioner of investigation for New York City schools, reports, "I don't want people to think there are massive hordes of child molesters in the schools, but it is certainly true that there are a lot of relationships between adolescents and school staff."[1]

Teacher misconduct is a problem that must be faced and solved. I believe the charge that there is an epidemic of such teacher behaviors is off the mark and, in fact, detrimental to solving the problem. Why? Because the cure put forth is often legalistic, focusing on teachers who are identified as sexual predators as the main culprits, implementing programs to screen and remove predator teachers with past records of misconduct and teacher training that simply gives them guidelines for avoiding sexual misconduct rather than the necessary skills.

This legalistic response heightens the anxiety of students, parents, community members, and teachers and may result in a negative school climate in which close contact between teachers and students is suspect. Often it gives rise to vigilante groups. Such a climate discourages important and needed personal contact between teachers and students, erodes trust between teachers and students, erodes trust among colleagues in a school setting in which everyone is suspect, and erodes trust between teachers and parents who are already struggling to balance the innocence of childhood with a growing national awareness that the world is a dangerous place.

This legalistic "cure" can quickly cast a pall over an open and safe school environment when the newspaper headlines and TV talk shows cry out that there is an "epidemic of teacher sexual misconduct in America." This is not to suggest that there are no sexual predators in our schools. Clearly they must be identified early on, screened out, directed toward help, and dismissed before more harm is done to students. In addition, we need to broaden our training and intervention efforts to educate all teachers about the dangers of crossing professional boundaries and becoming involved in sexual misconduct with vulnerable students. An important mission of public schools is to care and protect students from harm and that pledge must be honored.

One-on-one relations between educators and students found in teaching, mentoring, coaching, advising, drama and theater, and club leadership often provide fertile territory for relationships to move into close friendship. For example, chapter 3 provides an example of the mischief that can occur as a result of the impact of the early 1970s Title IX legislation that spawned a wave of new sports teams for young women, coached by male faculty members who had no training in how to manage close one-on-one contact with young women.

There are sexual predators in schools, but that is not the whole story of sexual misconduct by teachers. The majority of teachers who become involved in sexual misconduct are at-risk individuals with home, work, and emotional problems. Unfortunately many become involved in close one-on-one contact with students for which they have no preparation, supervision, training, and no open doors of help that they can enter before their acting out behavior brings harm to vulnerable students, behaviors that are out of bounds for any professional and that they will be blamed for, facing the probability of abuse charges and jail time.

They are on their own in dangerous territory, as are their at-risk students. They fail to see the red light of danger trying to warn them off crossing professional boundaries and become at risk of becoming a friend, parent figure, and even a lover for a student.

The cases describe in chapters 2 through 4 include a pattern of looking the other way by colleagues, administrators, students, and parents. They observe teachers engaging in risky behaviors but they, like the at-risk teachers involved, lack the skills for confronting the situation. We need to train administrators, teacher leaders, and teachers to demystify the notion that "it can't happen here" and "it can't happen to me" and provide the training they need.

The root of the vast majority of incidents involving teacher sexual misconduct then lies in the lack of training, supervision, monitoring, and intervention for teachers who have not learned how to establish clear professional boundaries and don't see a red light of danger when they cross professional boundaries and become personally involved with students, many who are at risk and searching for a caring adult role model they do not have at home.

We need to raise the awareness of educators that it is risky to help adolescents resolve personal issues without ongoing training, supervision, monitoring, and intervention.

As Dr. Ava L. Siegler, director of the Institute for Child, Adolescent, and Family Studies in New York City, suggests, "all adolescents are vulnerable. They are looking for someone to emulate and seeking approval. Yet psychologically they may not be ready to deal with the consequences of physical and emotional intimacy."[2]

THIS BOOK WILL PROVIDE ANSWERS TO THE FOLLOWING QUESTIONS REGARDING THE ISSUES INVOLVED IN SEXUAL MISCONDUCT IN ORDER TO HELP ADMINISTRATORS, TEACHER LEADERS, UNION LEADERS, PARENTS, AND COMMUNITY MEMBERS BE BETTER PREPARED IN PLANNING SUCCESSFUL EFFORTS TO CURTAIL SEXUAL MISCONDUCT IN THEIR SCHOOLS.

Sexual misconduct can happen in any school given the combination of at-risk teachers in need of personal contact and needy students looking for an adult mentor and model. As researcher and psychologist Jan Kinder Mathews suggests, "When you have a needy child and a needy adult, that's just abuse waiting to happen."[3] We need to shine new light on sexual misconduct in order to offer the needed protection for students. The goals of this book are to answers these questions and better prepare administrators, teacher leaders, coaches, union leaders, parents, and community members to mount effective training and intervention efforts.

1. What behaviors represent teacher sexual misconduct?

2. What are the personal and professional conditions that can spawn such behavior?

3. Why have the discussions about teacher sexual misconduct been limited to the legal aspects involved, discussions that focus solely on the teachers involved as sexual predators and ignore the reality that there are at-risk teachers in our schools with personal and professional troubles in their lives who cross professional boundaries and try to form personal connections and relationships with at-risk students who are also experiencing personal troubles at home and in school.

4. Why has framing sexual misconduct primarily as acts carried out by predators and psychotic teachers who need to be weeded out shifted the remedy away from where the real problem lies: providing effective training, supervision, and monitoring for all teachers? We need a broader, more inclusive definition of which teachers are at risk for sexual misconduct.

5. We need to acknowledge that some predator teachers exist in our schools and closely study why they often go undetected. For example, why is it that the climate in some school settings creates conditions in which highly successful, powerful teachers and coaches are able to prey on vulnerable students and ignore boundaries and professional standards without supervision, monitoring, confrontation, intervention, and dismissal?

6. Why is it that in many cases of teacher sexual misconduct the student victims who come forward are discounted, threatened into silence, and perceived as troublemakers out to ruin the reputation of the school and the teachers involved in the misconduct? Why is it that the institutional reaction is often to destroy the messenger?

7. What are the costs to the teacher and students involved, their families, colleagues, peers, and the school district?

8. How can training, supervision, monitoring, and quick intervention help teachers understand the hazards and risks involved and avoid misconduct? How can colleagues and administrators intervene when they observe a teacher becoming involved in risky relationships that are evident to all members of the school community?

THE COMMON DENOMINATOR BETWEEN EDUCATORS, PHYSICIANS, AND CATHOLIC PRIESTS WHO BECOME INVOLVED IN SEXUAL MISCONDUCT

Sexual misconduct occurs in every profession that brings caregivers into close contact with needy youth, such as physicians, priests, and educators. As seen in the recent revelations concerning Catholic priests, when training, supervision, monitoring, and intervention is absent, there can be tragic consequences for those they are sworn to help. For example, a look at the sexual misconduct of physicians offers an important beginning to understanding how sexual misconduct can emerge in the lives of seemingly healthy caregivers.

In the study "Sexual Boundaries and Physicians: Overview and Educational Approach to the Problem," researcher William Swiggart and colleagues at Vanderbilt University Medical Center suggest that sexual misconduct may include inappropriate sexual comments and initiation of conversations regarding sexual problems, preferences, or fantasies.[4]

Swiggart also cites the following research by G. O. Gabbard and colleagues:[5]

> The family history of physicians involved in sexual misconduct often reflects a lack of clear boundaries. These include an array of childhood trauma experiences from distant and neglectful parenting.

Physicians who have difficulty refusing requests for after-hours appointments and meetings are at risk of sexual misconduct.

Most physicians who cross sexual boundaries are older and well established in practice.

They fail to have clear office policies with the absence of dress codes and excessive familiarity with nurses and staff that impairs the professional atmosphere.

Gabbard and Swiggart's data suggest that, like physicians, many of the teachers involved in sexual misconduct are not predators or psychotics. Yes, predators and psychotic teachers do exist and we must keep these teachers away from students and out of our schools. But the majority of teachers involved in sexual misconduct, like physicians, fall into the category of at-risk teachers who are experiencing a life crisis such as a divorce, death or illness of a spouse, child, or family member, poor health, or professional failure, and seek relationships with and needy and at-risk students.

The majority of teachers involved in sexual misconduct are teachers who become overly involved with students, often seeking out students who are going through some of the same difficult problems these teachers experienced as teens, such as divorce, alcohol and drug abuse by parents, abandonment, physical abuse, social isolation, lack of friends, and living in poverty.

These savior-teachers think they can save their students from the same pain they felt as children, and in the saving process they take on the role of a surrogate parent, mentor, friend, and sometimes lover. Some of these teachers were raised by distant and neglectful parents.

AN EDUCATOR SUFFERING FROM CAREER BURNOUT AND BOREDOM CAN BE VULNERABLE TO BECOMING INVOLVED IN SEXUAL MISCONDUCT

However, this book takes note that some of the teachers described in the case studies in chapter 2, while at-risk individuals, are also professionals who have made it, becoming good at what they do and successful in their careers. Without new challenges, professional caregivers like physicians and teachers can become bored and seek excitement in personal relationships. These can be teachers who are stars, looked up to by colleagues, students, and parents. As one teacher told me, "Who would have thought that Dennis, chair of his department, good family life, wonderful kids, would get personally involved with a student? I guess he was just looking for some change, excitement."

ADMINISTRATORS, TEACHERS, COUNSELORS, STUDENTS, AND PARENTS OFTEN DISTANCE THEMSELVES FROM INTERVENING WHEN THEY OBSERVE CASES OF SEXUAL MISCONDUCT. IT'S NOT SUPPOSED TO HAPPEN IN THEIR SCHOOL

There is a lot of looking the other way in schools by educators who are untrained to intervene when they see colleagues crossing boundaries. As the research by *Education Week* on sexual misconduct by school employees from March through August 1998 suggests,[6] many educators are wearing blinders, holding on to false assumptions, and resisting the creation of more openness/awareness that this kind of activity "can happen here" and the implementation of needed training, supervision, monitoring, and intervention. Here are some of the report's findings.

Such behavior happens in all kinds of schools: public and private, religious and secular, rural and urban, rich and poor. Often the setting is in the school building or in cars, motel rooms, or the student's or employee's home.

The feeling that sexual misconduct by teachers is not supposed to happen in our district is the dominant theme in school life. As Wayne Huagen, the superintendent of the Hastings, Minnesota, schools, suggests, "In the back of your mind, you know that anything is possible but you don't expect it to occur." A female teacher in Hastings pleaded guilty to sexual misconduct in July 1998 after a four-month sexual relationship with a teenage student. Huagen said, "It's something that always happens in some other part of the country or in some other school district."

Often the teachers involved are the most popular and dedicated in the school. In New Tier High School in Winnetka, Illinois, a social studies teacher who was voted the "most liked male teacher" was suspended for fondling a sixteen-year-old girl.

Teachers involved as leaders in extracurricular activities such as music, drama, and athletics were more likely to be involved in sexual misconduct with students.

Colleagues and administrators are often reluctant to come forward when they suspect something is amiss in teacher–student relationships, such as crossing boundaries even when the acting out behavior is obvious.

TELLING THE TRUTH ABOUT SEXUAL MISCONDUCT— IT CAN HAPPEN IN YOUR SCHOOL

Talking to educators about sexual misconduct in general terms without putting a real face on the problem and the personal/professional complications involved in setting safe boundaries can lull educators and parents into thinking these kinds of acts are always abnormal and are carried out, as common lore suggests, only by predators. Addressing these kinds of acting-out behaviors can help us understand where our training, supervision, monitoring, and intervention efforts need to be focused.

The following films clearly point out what can happen to teachers as they become involved in or are on the road to sexual misconduct. In these films, the profile of professionals at risk for sexual misconduct clearly emerges.

For example, neither of the two teachers has been trained in how to establish clear sexual boundaries. While appearing healthy, they are experiencing significant life crises in their out-of-school relationships, they are tireless and selfless in their devotion to needy students, they have difficulty in refusing requests for after-hours appointments, and they are older and well established in their teaching roles.

No, these films are not professional case studies. But they help us come in contact with the real feelings, the human needs, the physical attractions, and the moral dilemmas that come with the desire to be honorable professionals versus the need to connect with a student on a personal level in order to escape from the personal and professional troubles in their own lives. Unfortunately it's a dangerous and risky path to follow and often results in harm and abuse for the student involved and dismissal for the teacher.

The film *Carried Away* chronicles the professional and personal dilemmas of Joseph, played by Dennis Hopper, a teacher whose days are spent educating children in a Midwestern farm town.[7] At night he cares for his terminally ill mother. He is in the caring business day and night. He has an on-and-off relationship with Rosalee, a teacher who is struggling to raise her teenage son alone. Despite her numerous declarations of love and her desire to get married, Rosalee cannot get through to Joseph, who keeps his emotions locked up. Things change rapidly when Joseph becomes involved with Catherine, a radiant seventeen-year-old student.

Joseph discovers his reservoir of feelings for the first time, experiencing a degree of passion and vitality he never thought possible. As film director Bruno Barreto comments, "You have Joseph, a man leading a sedate life in a dead-end relationship with Rosalee, his childhood sweetheart. However events bring a Catherine, seventeen-year-old girl, into his class as a student. They start an affair that turns the whole community upside down, but it awakens within him a passion that ultimately resuscitates his relationship with Rosalee."

The film questions all of the concepts of right and wrong in terms of contemporary morality. Joseph is not a sexual deviant out to prey on vulnerable teens. Instead it appears that he's involved in too much caring for others, such as his students and his dying mother, and is unable to find affection for himself with Rosalee, his longtime sweetheart.

The pattern that evolves in Joseph and Catherine's relationship is consistent with how many sexual misconduct cases begin in our schools. It begins with untrained teachers who are needy for contact, little or no supervision or monitoring, and looking the other way by colleagues and administrators when it is obvious professional boundaries are being crossed.

When the affair comes to light it turns the community upside down. Everyone seems surprised and outraged at a drama that was clearly obvious, yet no one acted early on to stop the affair by confronting Joseph and guiding him into needed intervention as well as intervention for Catherine and her family.

Some of the same conditions, the impact of a life spent caring for others and developing a sense of vulnerability that spills over when an attractive student enters the picture, can be seen in the film *Mr. Holland's Opus*. Glen Holland (Richard Dreyfuss), a composer and professional musician, takes a teaching job in the newly renamed John F. Kennedy High School. Holland spent several years on the road as a musician but now is married.[8] His dream is to spend a few years teaching in order to accumulate enough savings to allow him to return to his true passion in life: composing music.

However, events soon change everything. His wife, Iris, becomes pregnant, and in order to provide for her and their new son, Cole, Holland finds himself having to settle down, buy a house, become a music teacher during the school year, and teach driver education in the summer to make ends meet. At first Glen is not enamored with his life as a teacher. For him teaching is just a means to earn money.

However, as Ransom Fellowship film reviewer Rick Mattson points out, Holland breaks through to disinterested students by employing radical teaching techniques in the face of conservative opposition, then exercises profound influence on selected underdog students.[9] He convinces his students that playing music is supposed to be fun. His extra work pays dividends in the music program at Kennedy High School, creating a loyal following of students.

However, although Holland is achieving professional success at Kennedy, he is experiencing growing personal problems at home. His son Cole is found to be deaf and must have special training and schooling. Much of this responsibility is placed on Iris. The fact that Cole cannot hear makes it difficult for father and son to relate to each other. Tensions rise between Glenn and Iris as they try to adjust to the challenges of finding the best care for Cole. Glenn has a greater involvement in school activities such as directing the annual school musical, and Iris spends more and more time alone. The marriage is in trouble.

Holland has relationship problems with his wife and is on unsure ground with his son. Glenn is not seeking other female relationships, but he is increasingly lonely and emotionally removed from his home. As he grows distant and perfunctory at home, he finds himself at school in stimulating working relationships with talented students, among them Rowena, a beautiful, talented twelfth-grade star of the school musical, who mesmerizes him.

However, unlike Joseph, Glenn Holland knows the hazards and risks involved in developing a personal relationship with a student, but heading off a disastrous relationship isn't easy. Glenn is getting a lot of personal gratification out of mentoring Rowena. It seems easier for him to be the center of Rowena's interest than to deal with the festering problems at home. He doesn't have a trusted colleague or administrator to help him sort out his conflicted feelings. He has to do it on his own and make the difficult choice to say goodbye to Rowena and return home to deal with saving his marriage and finding ways to relate to his son.

Mr. Holland's Opus vividly portrays how mentors with unresolved personal problems can become involved with needy students. However, in this case Glenn is lucky, as is Rowena. He is not naïve about the dangers and risks involved for him, his family, and Rowena, and he is able to put on the brakes before mischief happens. But many teachers lack Holland's awareness and ability to confront the situation. As Mattson suggests, those of us involved in teaching know that it is a noble but sometimes tragic calling. Teachers cannot completely distance themselves emotionally from pupils' lives. The pressure of teaching can be massive in the workplace and, as we see through Glenn Holland, at home as well.

PLACING EDUCATORS IN CLOSE CONTACT WITH STUDENTS WITHOUT TRAINING CAN LEAD TO INVOLVEMENT IN SEXUAL MISCONDUCT

The combination of untrained teachers without adequate supervision and monitoring is risky business. Well-intentioned teachers intent on doing good and caring for students often don't see the hazards and risks involved before it's too late. But there is more to the story. Beginning in the late 1980s, there has been a rising drumbeat at the national level to have secondary teachers become mentors, advisers, and advocates for students who lack positive adult mentors. They are urged to embrace the concept that their mission needs to be expanded from the role of an academic teacher to include helping students resolve nonacademic problems that may be impacting negatively on their school success and personal well-being. It was at this time that the issue of teachers possibly becoming involved in sexual misconduct with their needy students arose.

The issue of sexual misconduct often hits home for teachers when they become involved in programs to train secondary school teachers to serve as advisers and personal adult advocates for students. For example, the 1989 publication of *Turning Points: Preparing American Youth for the 21st Century* called for teachers to serve as advisers and forge helping and personal relations with students.[10] *Turning Points* recommended that every student be well known by at least one adult in the school. Students should be able to rely on that adult to help them learn from their experiences, comprehend physical changes and changing relationships with family and peers, and act on their behalf to marshal every school and community resource needed for the student to succeed.

In 2000 a follow-up book, *Turning Points 2000: Educating Adolescents in the 21st Century*, continued to advocate for an important role for teachers as advisers by suggesting that when students make a lasting connection with at least one caring adult, academic and personal outcomes improve.[11] A significant adult who provides support and direction during difficult times can help students avoid academic failure and a variety of other problems.

Turning Points 2000 concludes that among youth at risk from health or behavioral problems, family dysfunction, poverty, and other stress, the most important school factor for fostering resiliency may be the availability of at least one caring responsible adult who can function as a mentor and role model. *Turning Points: Preparing American Youth for the 21st Century* and *Turning Points 2000: Educating Adolescents in the 21st Century* highlighted the need for students to connect with caring adult role models to help them navigate through the ups and downs of adolescent life and the important role of teachers in helping students resolve their nonacademic as well as academic problems.

The National Association of Secondary School Principals' 1996 report *Breaking Ranks: Changing an American Institution*[12] and the 2004 report *Breaking Ranks II: Strategies for Leading High School Reform*[13] echoed similar recommendations suggesting every high school student have a personal adult advocate to help him or her personalize the educational experience.

The *Breaking Ranks II* report suggested that teachers who serve as personal adult advocates will convey a sense of caring so that their students feel that their teacher shares a stake in their learning. The aspirations, strengths, and weaknesses of each student are known by at least one faculty member, and this will aid in engaging students' families as partners in education.

There were other powerful forces at work encouraging teachers to have closer contact with students to help them resolve both academic and nonacademic problems. As the *Public Agenda* report "Kids These Days: What Americans Really Think about the Next Generation"[14] suggests, Americans think these are uniquely difficult times for kids. More than eight in ten (83 percent) say it's harder to be a kid growing up in America today.

For example, Americans are extremely concerned about threats endangering all kids: drugs and crime, sex and violence in the media, and public schools that often fail to deliver education in a safe and orderly way. Yet as the report suggests, Americans refuse to give up on kids. They care deeply about their well-being and believe that tackling the issue is of paramount importance to society. Most encouraging, they are stubbornly optimistic about the chances of reclaiming the lives of even the most troubled teens. Americans demonstrate surprisingly high levels of caring and sympathy toward young people. In fact, Americans display an extraordinary, almost stubborn, refusal to write young people off as unsalvageable.

Almost three-quarters (72 percent) of Americans say that "given enough love and kindness, just about any kid can be reached." Even the toughest youngsters, teenagers already in deep trouble, can be redeemed given the right amount of effort. And 74 percent say that given help and attention, just about all youngsters can succeed in school. Teachers were looked to as the main players in salvaging troubled students by refusing to give up on them, providing the right effort to help these students reclaim their lives, demonstrating care and sympathy, and giving them help and attention so that they can learn and succeed in school.

In a sense teachers were encouraged to take on a quasi-savior role, again without training in the hazards and risks involved and how to communicate on a nonacademic, personal level that has clear boundaries.

The rush to have teachers save students from dropping out and facing a diminished future also gained momentum with changing economic, cultural, and social problems happening at the national level. For example, with the increase in family mobility and immigration, it became all too easy for newcomer students to get lost and lose out on a sense of safety, continuity, and belonging when moving into larger secondary schools.

Teachers on the front lines were the best positioned to intervene and guide these students. And the American family was undergoing great changes with the increase in divorce rates and one-parent families, the decline in enrollment in church programs, school PTAs, community groups, and other sources of trust and support, the pressure of time and money including the special pressures on two-career families and lack of opportunity for families to eat and play together, and mounting isolation from positive community influences.

We became a nation on the move with less time for child rearing and nurturing. Teachers were pushed into the breach to serve as positive adult role models for students who were often home alone, caring for younger siblings, and unsupervised. The role of teacher increasingly included being a mentor, adviser, and advocate. But again, teachers were propelled into these roles without training and a clear vision of how to proceed. They knew how to be academic teachers. Students come in, they take their seats, and the teacher teaches, more often than not by lecture.

But teachers wondered how they could meet one-on-one with students, encourage them to talk about personal issues, seek help when the student's life story was beyond their helping skills, and be available when needy students need attention. Questions abound. Should I give students my phone number? Should I meet with them outside of school? How do I refer students who are clearly troubled, even suicidal? How do I help a student who is being neglected or abused?

When teachers responded to administrators' requests to have increased personal contact with students, they often said, "I'm not trained for this kind of work." And they were right. The intention to have teachers serve as mentors, advisers, and advocates was admirable, but good intentions were not enough. Without training, two things seemed clear. First, many teachers would fail in their efforts to develop close contact with students. Yes, they might be given the title of "adviser," but over time would lack the skills necessary to be effective in this role, a losing situation for both teacher and student.

And on a more risky scale, some teachers might become involved in personal contact that was outside professional boundaries, such as meeting a student for dinner, giving gifts and money, visiting students after hours at their home, and so on, placing themselves and their students in harm's way.

Professional conditions that arise from well-intentioned recommendations to alter in a positive way how teachers interact with students can spawn teacher sexual misconduct. The problem is not the worthy and needed recommendations for knowing our students well, but in the failure to prepare teachers for the tasks and hazards involved. As a result, when it came time to implement the recommendations of the *Turning Points* and *Breaking Ranks* reports—for teachers to become more involved with their students and serve as adult role models in order to overcome the increasing absence of parents from the home due to the changing economic landscape—there was often little direction on how to move from their primary role as academic teachers into a mentoring, advising, and advocating role.

There were two major problems for teachers as they proceeded into this new career alternative. First, as researcher Pedro A. Noguera points out in a study of reform efforts in ten Boston high schools, the schools' attempts to personalize schooling through an advisory system in which teachers served as student counselors during an extended homeroom period held once a week seemed ineffective.[15]

Noguera reports, "We sat in on several advisory classes where no advising was occurring. The teachers had no idea how to use the allotted time and most lack experience in counseling." Good ideas, such as having teachers take on advisory roles, quickly flounder without follow up and training. This is a losing situation for students in need of positive adult connections and for teachers who need to learn how to proceed and be successful as advisers.

Second, the lack of training as advisers can also create problems. If teachers do not fully understand their professional boundaries, it can lead to trouble for teachers who are at risk of sexual misconduct with students. While some teachers, as the Noguera study suggests, resist taking on the role of adviser and continue to maintain their social distance from the personal side of the complex, tangled, and sometimes destructive lives of their students, others will rush into the adviser role and become overly involved with their students.

The boundary between helping and becoming a friend, confidante, surrogate parent, even a lover is hard to see when teachers become overly involved with their students. Sexual issues and needs dominate teenage life, as do the needs to belong, be accepted, be cared for, and be loved. When teenage students find a caring teacher, sometimes they transfer those feelings to that person. Teachers have similar needs for friendship, to be cared for and accepted.

Those needy and troubled teachers involved in sexual misconduct often fail to remember they are first professionals with the primary mission of educating, caring, and protecting their students from harm. Yes, many teachers will experience issues related to divorce, death of loved ones, parenting, failure in the classroom, career setbacks, addictions, family dysfunction, and issues of poor health and aging, like everyone else. Events in their personal lives can trigger the need for affection, friendship, and close contact with students. But these issues and events do not give them permission and license to become involved in sexual misconduct with their students.

As a beginning work on teacher sexual misconduct suggests, a 1996 *Fastback* for Phi Delta Kappa,[16] sometimes the personal needs of students and teachers converge when they are involved in an adviser–advisee helping role that often involves one-on-one discussions of emotions in which students may share intimate thoughts and feelings that can provide teachers with insights into their problems and motivation for learning. If a teacher's own personal needs for love and affirmation become thwarted, he or she may unfortunately seek to meet these needs through a close involvement with a needy student, a student looking for an adult role model whom he or she sees on a regular basis.

This is a potentially explosive situation for both teachers and students headed toward the margins of school life, looking for connection and comfort. In my experience in training teachers, when teachers say, "I am not trained to help students with their personal problems," they are usually on target.

Teachers who dive into advising students without training are a threat to themselves and to students if they cross professional boundaries and become involved in sexual misconduct, damaging the lives of their students and the families they are trying to help, as well as their own career and personal lives. They are also a threat to the important work of many well-trained teachers who serve as successful advisers and know their boundaries when involved in helping students in need of positive adult contact. As the saying goes, one bad apple can spoil the rest.

Given the reality that any teacher, under the right combination of circumstances, can find him- or herself heading toward the margins of school life and at risk of sexual misconduct, why is it that the major focus on the problem has been educating students and parents to report possible sexual offenses, hire more investigators to scrutinize teachers' behavior, conduct criminal background checks, and weed out sexual predators and psychotic teachers?

THE ARGUMENT FOR MORE TRAINING FOR EDUCATORS VERSUS A LEGALISTIC APPROACH TO CURTAILING SEXUAL MISCONDUCT

Why is there so little emphasis put on training teachers to prepare them for close personal contact and to be aware of the hazards and risks involved? Here is an example of how the sexual misconduct issue is being framed by administrators across the country.

David P. Driscoll, commissioner of education in Massachusetts, suggests that schools need to act more vigilantly to protect students from sexual misconduct by educators. Calling for increased scrutiny, Driscoll told *Boston Globe* reporter Anand Vaishnav that school districts have not paid enough attention to the problem.[17] Sexual misconduct is the primary reason that Massachusetts educators lose or surrender their teaching licenses.

Even so, the number of teachers disciplined for sexual misconduct accounts for less than 1 percent of the state's 72,000 public school teachers. The commissioner said he wants school districts to work harder to make students feel comfortable enough to report a possible sexual offense by a teacher or another adult in the school.

The state defines sexual misconduct as a range of activities that include verbal harassment, improper correspondence with a student, physical abuse, or inappropriate use of threats such as browsing adult websites or chat rooms. In his remarks, Driscoll said he plans to urge school boards to consider hiring more staff to investigate cases. He also wants to push for legislation tightening background checks on applicants.

Driscoll said he was spurred to do more by recent high-profile cases of alleged abuse by teachers. A middle school teacher in Chelmsford pleaded guilty to raping one of her students, and a high school teacher in Dudley was placed on leave after pleading not guilty to inducing a minor to have sex. In

Florida, Massachusetts, a middle school teacher was charged with having sex with a fourteen-year-old boy.

Driscoll reports, "We're seeing more and more instances, so we have to recognize that they may be there." In the past six years, the Department of Education has revoked, suspended, or denied twenty-six teaching certificates because of sexual misconduct. Those cases ranged from suggestive e-mails to a physical relationship.

Driscoll is right about the need for school leaders to put more emphasis on combating sexual misconduct by educators. However, unfortunately nowhere in this reported account is there any mention of emphasizing and budgeting training teachers on how to carry on close contact with students while avoiding sexual misconduct. It's all about vigilance, reporting, investigating, and the legal aspects of the issue.

There is nothing in the report about how the teachers in Chelmsford, Dudley, and Florida were swept along into such risky and acting out behaviors. Nor is there any description of the twenty-six teachers who lost their teaching certificates due to sexual misconduct. Some of these teachers may indeed have been predators or psychotics. Or were they untrained professionals caught in circumstances they were unprepared to handle?

But what is clear, and Driscoll says it well, is, "We're seeing more and more instances (of sexual misconduct) so we just have to recognize that they may be there." Driscoll is right in suggesting that "they may be there," but he, at least in this interview, places all his bets on vigilance, investigations, and background checks. However, the plan he promotes still leaves teachers unprepared and without the supervision and monitoring they need.

Rather than fostering the notion that any teacher is at risk of sexual misconduct and opening up the discussion to increase administrator, teacher, parent, and community awareness, he takes the law enforcement view, not the training view, which often forces teachers into not risking close relationships with their students and closing their classroom doors, reducing trust among teachers, reducing trust between students/parents and teachers, encouraging negative labels and isolating teachers who continue to be personally involved with their students, and causing changes in the school environment from a safe and trusting climate into one of increased vigilance and suspicion, an environment that spawns divisions among teachers and leaves them ripe for accusations.

In fact, the events in Massachusetts crystallize the hazards and risks involved when teachers are expected to take on the role of adviser and provide students with a more personalized learning environment without the necessary training. On one hand, the dismissal of teachers in the schools of Chelmsford, Dudley, and Florida for sexual misconduct is met with a call for more vigilance, scrutiny, and background checks for teachers. Yet at the same time teachers in some Boston high schools are expected to serve as advisers, quasi-counselors for students, with minimal or no training.

Here are two very different approaches. One says to watch all teachers' close involvement with students as it can lead to sexual misconduct. The other says we need to have teachers become more personally involved with students and help them resolve personal, family, and health and well-being problems.

One approach says to teachers, "Be careful and stay away from close contact." The other says, "Close contact is now part of your role." These two approaches characterize the ways in which schools approach how teachers should interact with students on a personal level. Both approaches are flawed as neither includes the need to train, supervise, and monitor teachers or the notion that every teacher, given the right combination of personal and professional circumstances, is at risk for sexual misconduct. It is a subject that is either not talked about or framed only as an act by predators and psychotics.

Again, a look at research by Pedro Noguera helps shed some light on the negative impact of teachers' lack of training in carrying on close relationships with students. Noguera reports that the effort in ten Boston high schools to create an advisory system to increase personal schooling and to raise student achievement was ineffective because of a lack of training. The teachers had no idea how to use the time made available through an extended homeroom period held once a week. Most lack experience in advising and counseling.

As Noguera suggests, considering the gap between idea and implementation, it is hardly surprising that small learning communities and advisory groups had not improved teacher–student relationships. Boston teachers did not receive even minimal training in how to be advisers. For example, how to carry on helping conversations, guide students to creditable resources in the school and community to deal with personal, family, and health and well-being problems, be advocates for students with fellow teachers and administrators, and, most of all, how to set boundaries with students.

Think of the hazards and risks waiting for the teachers and their students in large urban high schools where, as Noguera describes, pervasive student alienation, boredom, strained relationships between adults and students, and a dropout rate often above 50 percent are present. These are adolescents, many needy and troubled and headed for dropping out, seeking advice and a personal connection with advisers who lack training and experience. Maybe sexual misconduct didn't happen in any of the teacher adviser–student contacts, but the opportunities for such boundary crossing were clearly present.

Many of the good ideas of the *Turning Point* and *Breaking Ranks* reports resulted in failed efforts because of poor implementation. The Boston teachers, it appears, were sent off on a mission without being well prepared, as perhaps the teachers from Chelmsford, Dudley, and Florida were.

However, many advocates for curtailing sexual misconduct in the schools have given low priority to utilizing training, supervision, monitoring, and quick intervention. For example, a draft report by researcher Charol Shakeshaft commissioned for the U.S. Department of Education says, "There are practices that many believe are likely to reduce educator sexual misconduct." Here are some of Shakeshaft's recommendations as described in *Education Week*:

> Craft written policies that unambiguously describe and prohibit inappropriate educator–student relationships.
>
> Screen new and current employees with background checks that include fingerprinting.
>
> Centralize record keeping and designate one case coordinator to whom "all rumors, allegations, or complaints are channeled."
>
> Make educators, parents, and students aware of the signs of misconduct by educators.
>
> Educate employees and students about expectations for behavior, the responsibility to report suspected wrongdoing, and the proper channels for doing so.
>
> Change state certification rules to require new educators to "understand the professional expectations and ethics in regard to student relationships."
>
> Set up adequate state and federal registries of educators who have engaged in sexual misconduct with students "where future employers or parents can turn to check backgrounds."
>
> Revise state policies to protect students of all ages, to require stringent background checks, to mandate reporting to the state of misconduct accusations, and so on.[18]

Not unlike David Driscoll's recommendations, Shakeshaft's focus is on written policies, screening, background checks, and investigations, educating students and parents to be aware of the "signs" of sexual misconduct, and educating professionals about behavioral expectations. However, Shakeshaft adds another controversial recommendation: implementing a centralized record-keeping system and designating a case coordinator to whom "all rumors, allegations, or complaints are channeled."

Again, what is missing in the report is the need for effective training, supervision, and monitoring of all teachers. Rather, the report emphasizes vigilance, screening, and investigation that would establish a climate in which every teacher is suspect and vulnerable to charges that would increasingly flow secretly and unchallenged into a case coordinator's office from any member of the school community who has heard rumors or suspects misconduct.

POTENTIAL PROBLEMS WHEN SCHOOLS ONLY RELY ON A LEGALISTIC APPROACH TO CURTAILING SEXUAL MISCONDUCT

One wonders where the rights of teachers to defend themselves are before a case is secretly built against them. Where is the needed role of the school administrator in being the primary person responsible for supervising teachers? Where is the needed role of teacher union representatives in protecting their members from rumors, possibly false accusations, and complaints?

There is a place for screening and background checks to weed out sexual predators and psychotic teachers. But that effort can also create a school climate that focuses on vigilance and suspicion, and welcomes rumor, allegations, and labeling that may be false, premature, and in some cases a vendetta against a given teacher.

We need to make sure that our remedy to the problem of sexual misconduct doesn't result in a less trusting, safe, supportive, and caring environment for both students and teachers. Some educators took issue with Shakeshaft's finding that more than 4.5 million students endure sexual misconduct in their schools.[19] Shakeshaft says that the best estimate available shows that 10 percent of children face teacher misbehavior, from unprofessional to criminal, between kindergarten and twelfth grade.

Paul Houston, executive director of the American Association of School Administrators, said, "Out of the millions of teachers out there, you're talking about a very small number who are doing inappropriate things. Teachers increasingly fear making even the most innocent gesture, such as hugging a child who is having a bad day." The National Education Association (NEA), the American Federation of Teachers (AFT), and the National School Boards Association (NSBA) all said the report could create a false impression in the public's mind that the physical sexual abuse of students by educators is rampant in schools.[20] The NEA called the report's tone alarmist, and the NSBA suggested that it diminished the problem by appearing to overstate it.

Michael Pons, a spokesman for the NEA, said that the 2.7 million member union does not "dismiss the importance of eradicating sexual harassment in the schools," but is concerned about the report's broad focus. "Most people, especially parents, will not read the report and understand some of the nuances of it," he said. "Instead, they will hear that one in ten children is sexually abused in the schools." We need to heed the advice of the NSBA and not diminish the problem by overstating it, alarming educators, parents, and students, and masking the problem as a predator issue.

In reality, the issue requires upping the implementation ante by responding to the need for all teachers to be trained on how to have close contact with students and at the same time avoid the hazards and risks involved. As Paul Houston might say, the key is in knowing when a hug is appropriate to help a child who is having a bad day to refocus on school in a positive way. There is no mystery in making meaningful contact with students. Our words, our body language, and our gestures all spell inviting and caring on the one hand or negativity and no entry on the other. The danger comes when the intent of the contact may be a sign of a teacher crossing professional boundaries to establish a personal sexual misconduct relationship.

That's the kind of training I am promoting. Training that focuses on developing self-awareness among teachers and the sounding of an alarm when they cross professional boundaries and become overly involved in their students' personal lives. Training raises the expectation that when a teacher is observed crossing professional boundaries, colleagues and administrators will act quickly to intervene and offer guidance, confrontation when needed, sources of help and referral, and ongoing support to bring any evidence of sexual misconduct to an end.

Training that clearly identifies open doors in the school where teachers involved in possible sexual misconduct can find skilled professionals who can offer advice, counseling, and direction in a safe and trusting atmosphere; professionals who understand the heartaches that can visit students and their families, and the families of the at-risk teacher when sexual misconduct looms.

This model moves the dialogue about sexual misconduct from a secretive or "it can't happen here" context into an open discussion that places misconduct in the context it belongs: as a real problem that can happen to teachers who find themselves at risk due to professional and personal problems. We need to move the discussion of sexual misconduct away from the dark corners of school life where rumors thrive and admit that it can happen in our school and that it's better to have teachers well trained than to deny them the needed skills required for close contact with students.

We need to normalize the issue of sexual misconduct, not sweep it under the rug or promote the idea that only crazy teachers on the fringe of school life carry out such behaviors. We need to dispel the notion that there is an epidemic of teacher sexual misconduct in our schools. As clinical psychologist and sexologist Leonore Tieffer asserts, "A new concern for sexual misconduct arose in the 1980s. Although surveys attempted to assess the prevalence of sexual misconduct, they ran into trouble almost immediately. When is a hug sexual? A kiss? Is there a correct way to express caring? What about affection? How can you tabulate these things on a questionnaire?"[21]

Facing the problem of sexual misconduct in schools also requires attention to researcher Dan H. Wishnietsky's observation that "because of their status and position, educators have a rare opportunity to make a positive impact on the lives of students who may not have a positive role model elsewhere. High school students are impressionable and might possibly encourage improper relationships. At this point teachers must employ special caution by keeping all relationships totally professional."[22]

But simply talking about what teachers should do without arming them with the real-world skills to ready them to "employ special caution to keep all relationships totally professional" will never solve the problem of sexual misconduct in the absence of special training.

Just talking about how teachers should behave, giving them written policies and guidelines, and implementing some of Shakeshaft's recommendations, such as a case coordinator role in the schools, will have the negative impact of creating a climate for "all rumors, allegations, or complaints" and may actually invite false charges against teachers. This will ruin lives and professional careers and cast a dark cloud of suspicion over all student–teacher relationships.

Here are some examples of how the lives of dedicated teachers can be uprooted and sometimes ruined. After being accused by several students of sexually provocative behavior in a girls' locker room, gym teacher Roland Heller, of Montgomery County, Maryland, saw his career nearly destroyed in early 2000.[23] Suspended from work, he was given fifteen minutes to leave the school, threatened with arrest by the police, and labeled a sexual molester in the public eye. For almost a month, Heller's life was a virtual hell. But as time went by, police became suspicious about the students' stories. With each retelling, the youths embellished their accusations. It was discovered that the gym teacher had disciplined two of the students prior to the alleged incident. Finally a student confessed and the rest conceded the truth: they had made the whole thing up.

Today Heller is back in the classroom, but his exoneration has done little to reassure teachers familiar with his ordeal. In the back of their minds they wonder: Could an angry student falsely accuse me of wrongdoing? Would an investigation clear my name or drag it through the mud? As society aggressively tackles the problem of sexual harassment and abuse in the schools, increased awareness of the issue has given some students the idea that an accusation is a powerful weapon for mischief and revenge.

In 1994, Oregon teacher Dan Domenigoni was accused of inappropriately touching several junior high students, who also spread rumors of the charge throughout the school. The story made the television news and for seven weeks Domenigoni was the object of a police investigation. Finally his accusers recanted, admitting they had made up the story in the hope that the teacher would be fired.

James Corleto, a science teacher and girls' track coach at Freeport High School in New York State, presents another example of the damage that can happen to a teacher falsely charged with sexual misconduct. On July 21, 1998, Corleto was arrested on charges that he repeatedly fondled athletes.

The *Newsday* headline concerning the arrest was stark: "Track Coach Faces Molestation Charges: Female Ex-Athletes Report Fondling."[24] The abuse was alleged to have occurred dozens of times from July 1995 to May 1996 in Corleto's van. The students, who were under seventeen, have since graduated and only recently have told their stories, indicating that they "didn't want to talk about it" until now.

Corleto was not charged with sexual abuse because the alleged victims could not recall exact dates, but he was charged with two counts of endangering the welfare of a child, a misdemeanor punishable by up to a year in jail on conviction. The police indicated the allegations surfaced in the spring of 1998 when a former student athlete made reference to Corleto while e-mailing a former student over the Internet. Corleto's lawyer suggested that "imagination was at work. I think this was schoolgirl gossip that got out of control."

Corleto had been voted teacher of the year at Freeport in 1997, but was now arrested for fondling. Was Corleto's lawyer's assessment on target that "this was schoolgirl gossip that got out of control"? Evidently the jury agreed. It pondered the case for about an hour before reaching its verdict to clear Corleto of the two counts of endangering the welfare of a child.[25]

Yet false charges and labeling are hard to defend against. Our work is to prepare teachers for such a possibility the best we can. Part of our training, supervision, and monitoring to prevent sexual misconduct needs to include making teachers aware of the retaliatory power of students who are heading toward the margins of school life and have strained relationships with adults in their personal and school lives.

These students are capable of using aggressive acting-out behavior such as making charges of sexual misconduct. These kinds of charges by marginal students can find fertile ground in a school environment in which vigilance, suspicion, rumors, and false labeling of teachers form the chosen model for preventing sexual misconduct.

In the heated everyday exchanges and confrontations between teachers and students, sexual misconduct is only one of the many charges that can be falsely raised against teachers. Any teacher knows that in the open arena of school, one can be falsely labeled as incompetent, lazy, uncaring, unprepared, catering to favorite students, burned out, racist, too old, too young, too inexperienced, too aggressive, unable to discipline, and so on. It goes with the territory. Welcome to the club. Welcome to teaching in a secondary school in America. This territory requires teachers to know their students well and anticipate personal and professional attacks by some students and parents.

Teachers, then, need training in how to anticipate aggressive behavior by some students and not be naïve, surprised, and unprepared when they are falsely accused and tagged with a number of labels, including sexual misconduct. Students are not unaware of labeling and its powerful impact as they know from firsthand experience and observation of teacher–student relationships that students are often labeled as lazy, unprepared, spoiled, irresponsible, and so on.

Charges are easy to mount in secondary schools, both from students and teachers, and thrive in an environment in which trust is low and in which labeling is allowed to exist without a strong response by administrators and teachers, a response that sends a definite message that this kind of behavior has no place in a trusting school community.

Although researcher Shakeshaft says she has yet to uncover a deliberate case of lying and she's encountered only a handful of cases in which an accusation appeared to involve a student's misinterpretation of a teacher's action, Bruce Meredith, general counsel for the Wisconsin Education Association, disputes such contentions. He says he has been involved personally with numerous cases in which students later admitted they had lied. Meredith also raises the concern of false accusations that arise from misinterpretation rather than evil intent.

For example, a teacher could put a comforting arm around a shoulder and the student could view it as harassment. Meredith indicates, "Those are allegations where there's an enormous degree of unreliability in reporting. At worst, what you might find is some inappropriate decisions being made. The teacher might not be respecting the student's boundaries. But it's not criminal conduct."[26]

The bottom line is that in the often anonymous world of our large secondary schools, it is wise for both teachers and students to know where they are heading in teacher–student relationships. Not every teacher has the advantage of wisdom and support from caring colleagues who are willing to help and intervene. The same can be said of some students, who may not have parents who care and monitor their activities and peers who are ready to help and intervene.

There are needy teachers and students in search of close personal contact to make up for the loss of care, even love, in their lives. Sometimes, as in the case of teachers Heller and Domenigoni, there may be students whose parents and adult models have pushed them away, not been available to help when trouble came into their lives, and some who may be truly abandoned and alone.

As any experienced teacher knows, it is not uncommon for alienated students to transfer hostile and negative feelings they have toward parents onto unwitting teachers who don't see the anger and resentment coming. Not every teacher is experienced and savvy about such acting out students. Our work is to not let them remain naïve and unaware of the hazards and risks of close contact. It is critical that administrators and teacher leaders who are responsible for the professional development and well-being of teachers make sure their teachers are prepared to handle the various aspects of sexual misconduct and not become either victims or victimizers, preparations that were lacking in the sexual misconduct scandal in the Catholic Church.

For example, regarding Catholic priests, about one in ten of the alleged incidents of sexual abuse by priests in the United States over the past half-century took place in Catholic schools, with 5.1 percent occurring during school hours.[27] Among nearly 4,400 Catholic priests and deacons, 4 percent of priests were alleged to have committed such acts.

However, the Catholic Church's response has mainly involved background checks, not training for priests. The diocese of Rockville Center, Long Island, New York, began conducting background screening of clergy and other church personnel in the spring of 2004.[28] So far the diocese has completed a total of 22,571 background screenings of the priests, deacons, religious, lay staff, and volunteers who serve in diocesan agencies or any of the 134 parishes in the diocese.

The background screening is part of the diocese's larger effort, which includes training teachers, staff, and volunteers how to be on the alert for cases of sexual abuse and how to report it. Ellen Puglisi, director of the Diocesan Office for the Protection of Children and Young People, said, "The program helps make people aware of the warning signs that a child is being abused or a person is looking to abuse a child."

But here again we find no evidence that there is any effort to train priests, religious educators, and teachers on how to establish boundaries when they are involved in close contact with teens, nor any systematic effort to develop a supervision, monitoring, and intervention plan to head off sexual misconduct. The emphasis is on screening out predators who are sexual abusers, rather than training each person who is involved in offering care to troubled teens on how to avoid sexual misconduct.

That includes priests, teachers, and religious educators who are not, as Puglisi suggests, "looking to abuse a child," but are caregivers who find themselves involved in a close relationship that, as researcher Jane Kinder Matthews describes, involves a needy child and a needy adult. Troubled teens often turn to their church when they need help with personal issues such as divorce, a failed personal relationship, family illness or death, school and peer problems, or addictions. If they come in contact with untrained caregivers, harm and abuse can come their way.

Dr. Sylvester P. Theisen, professor emeritus of sociology at Saint John's College in Collegeville, Minnesota, reminds us that professional training programs for priests and religious educators remain as they always have been—negligent.[29] Hopefully this book will bring school leaders like David Driscoll on board and help them view the solution to teacher sexual misconduct as lying in effective training, supervision, and monitoring. Keep the legal means necessary to weed out the small number of sexual predators and psychotics, but begin to emphasize training, monitoring, and supervision as the cornerstones of an effective education and intervention plan.

AN OVERVIEW OF WHAT'S TO COME

Chapter 2 will focus on case studies of at-risk teachers who become involved in sexual misconduct relationships with needy students and how these cases might have been prevented. What is startling about these cases is how easy it was for teachers to drift into these relationships, lacking any training, supervision, or intervention. They were accidents waiting to happen.

Chapter 3 will focus on the risks involved in long-term, intensive, and intimate relations between educators and students, such as the kind that can be found in male faculty members coaching female athletes. This is fertile territory for relationships to move into close friendship and even love relations. This chapter provides a classic example of the mischief that can happen related to the impact of the Title IX in the early 1970s. It was a risky environment for sure, but school leaders and parents never saw the risks involved for teachers and students until the cases of sexual misconduct began to emerge, often with the victims being vilified and accused of a vendetta against successful, well-liked, and politically connected coaches who were community icons.

Chapter 4 will focus on cases of predator teachers and how these cases might also have been prevented. Again in these cases, what is startling is the lack of training, supervision, monitoring, intervention, and dismissal when these educators were clearly trying to lure and pressure vulnerable students into sexual activities.

Chapter 5 will present a training program administrators can implement to prepare teachers and coaches on how they can avoid sexual misconduct by creating clear boundaries with students. The chapter will also focus on how educators can pass on this training to teach students how they can establish clear boundaries in relationships with peers, teachers, coaches, and adult mentors.

The cases in each chapter clearly point out the need to provide adequate training for all teachers and the need to supervise and monitor teacher behavior and act quickly when behavior that is out of the norm appears.

NOTES

1. Edward Wyatt, "Schools Show Jump in Reports of Sex Abuse," *New York Times*, May 23, 2001, 1, 7 (B).

2. Margot Slade, "Yes, Statutory Rape Is Still a Rather Big Deal," *New York Times*, June 11, 1995, 9 (E).

3. Caroline Hendrie, "Abuse by Women Raises Its Own Set of Problems," *Education Week*, December 2, 1998, http://www.edweek.org/ew/vol-18/14women.h18.

4. William Swiggart, Karen Starr, Reid Finlayson, and Anderson Spickard, "Sexual Boundaries and Physicians: Overview and Education Approach to the Problem," Vanderbilt University Center for Professional Health, 2001, http://mc.vanderbilt.edu/root/vumc.php?site=cph&doc=742.

5. G. O. Gabbard, J. D. Bloom, C. C. Nadelson, and M. T. Norman, eds., *Psychodynamic Approaches to Physician Sexual Misconduct* (Washington, DC: American Psychiatric Press, 1999), 205–23.

6. Caroline Hendrie, "Sex with Students: When Employees Cross the Line," *Education Week*, December 2, 1998, http://www.edweek.org/ew/vol-18/14abuse.18.

7. Fine Line Features Synopsis, *Carried Away*, http://www.finelinefeatures.com/carried/synopsis.htm.

8. ChucksConnection Film Review, "Mr. Holland's Opus," http://www.chucksconnection.com/holland.html.

9. Rick Mattson, "Mr. Holland's Opus," http://ransomfellowship.org/M_MrHolland.html.

10. Carnegie Council on Adolescent Development: Task Force on Education of Young Adolescents, *Turning Points: Preparing American Youth for the 21st Century* (Washington, DC: Carnegie Council on Adolescent Development, 1989), 1–10.

11. Anthony W. Jackson and Gayle A. Davis, *Turning Points 2000: Educating Adolescents in the 21st Century* (New York: Teachers College Press, 2000), 140–44.

12. National Association of Secondary School Principals (NASSP), *Breaking Ranks: Changing an American Institution* (Reston, VA: National Association of Secondary School Principals, 1996), 1–20.

13. National Association of Secondary School Principals (NASSP), *Executive Summary of Breaking Ranks II: Strategies for Leading High School Reform* (Reston, VA: National Association of Secondary School Principals, 2004), 1–6.

14. Steve Farkas and Jean Johnson, "Kids These Days: What Americans Really Think about the Next Generation," *Public Agenda* (1999): 8–9, 11, 13, 16–19, 25–26.

15. Pedro A. Noguera, "Special Topics: Transforming High Schools," *Education Leadership*, May 2004, http://www.ascd.org/publications/ed_lead/200405/noguera.html.

16. William L. Fibkins, *Preventing Teacher Sexual Misconduct* (Bloomington, IN: Phi Delta Kappa Education Foundation, 1996), 8–9.

17. Anand Vaishnav, "Top Official Targets Abuse by Educators: Driscoll to Urge Vigilance," *Boston*, August 24, 2004, http://www.boston.com/news/local/articles/2004/08/24/top_official_targets_abuse_by_ed.

18. Caroline Hendrie, "Preventing Sexual Misconduct," *Education Week*, March 10, 2004, http://www.edweek.org/ew/ewstirt.cfm?slug=26abuse-B1.h23&keywords=sexual1%20ab.

19. Ben Feller, "Sexual Misconduct in Schools Tabulated," Associated Press, July 1, 2004, http://info/mgnetwork.com/printthispage.cgi?url=http%3A//222.tampatrib.com/news/M.

20. Caroline Hendrie, "Report Examining Sexual Misconduct Taps Some Nerves," *Education Week*, July 14, 2004, http://www.edweek.org/ew/ew_printstory.cfm>slug+42Abuse.h23.

21. Leonore Tieffer, "On the Therapist's Couch," *Newsday*, January 5, 1997, 37 (C).

22. Dan H. Wishnietsky, "Reported and Underreported Teacher–Student Sexual Harassment," *Journal of Education Research* 3 (1991): 164–69.

23. Del Stover, "What Happens When a Teacher Accused of Harassment Is Innocent?" *National School Boards Association*, May 16, 2000, http://nsba.org/site/print.asp?TRACKID=&VID=58&ATION=PRINT&CID=332&.

24. Blanca Monica Quintanilla, "Track Coach Faces Molestation Charges," *Newsday*, July 22, 1998, 29 (A).

25. Tom Demoretcky, "Teacher Cleared of Fondling," *Newsday*, January 26, 2000, 29 (A).

26. Stover, "What Happens When a Teacher Accused of Harassment Is Innocent?"

27. Mary Ann Zehr, "Report Tallies Alleged Sexual Abuse by Priests," *Education Week*, March 10, 2004, http://www.edweek.org/ew/ew_printstory.dfm?slug=26Catholic.h23.

28. Peter Sheehan, "Safety for All Is Goal of Background Screening, Training," *Long Island Catholic*, October 20, 2004, 1, 3.

29. Sylvester P. Theisen, "Interfaith Sexual Trauma Institute (ISTI) Book Review of John C. Gonsiorek, ed., *Breach of Trust: Sexual Exploration by Health Care Professionals and Clergy*," April 22, 1996, http://www.csbsju.edu/isti/Book%20Reviews/gonsiorek.html.

Chapter Two

Cases of Teachers Who Became Involved in Sexual Misconduct

What are the costs to teachers and students involved in sexual misconduct, their families, colleagues and administrators, parents, and the school district? In this chapter, the focus is case studies of teachers that illustrate the personal and professional costs involved and the inability of the school community to intervene when teachers are clearly moving into such risky behavior.

This chapter also uses data from these case studies to develop a profile of the kinds of teachers and students who may be at risk. One of the most compelling aspects of these case studies is the need both teachers and students have for an arena of comfort that is often missing in their personal lives.

As researchers Robert G. Simmons and Dale A. Blyth suggest, if the individual is comfortable in some environments, life arenas, and role relationships, the discomfort in another arena can be tolerated.[1] Students are less able to cope if at one and the same time they are uncomfortable with their changing bodies, changes in their family constellation, their home, a family move, moving to a larger school, their peers, sex relationships, or disrupted peer networks and changes in peer expectations and peer evaluation criteria.

There needs to be some arena of life or some set of role relationships with which the student can feel relaxed and comfortable, to which he or she can withdraw and be reinvigorated. As these case studies suggest, students looking for an arena of comfort because of negative changes in their family life, home situation, and peer relationships often look to teachers for such comfort.

However, in searching for such an arena of comfort, students sometimes connect with teachers who are untrained in close and personal contact with needy students and are themselves troubled by similar issues in their own lives; for example, deteriorating personal relationships, divorce, caring for ill family members, loneliness and isolation, disinterest and boredom with teaching, aging, and poor health.

These teachers may be looking for an arena of life or a set of role relationships with which they can feel relaxed and comfortable, to which they can withdraw and become reinvigorated, as is clearly demonstrated in the character of Joseph in the film *Carried Away*. This pairing of needy, at-risk students with untrained and at-risk teachers can be a toxic mix, a relationship that begins with good intentions and barrels into dangerous territory, a relationship that is observed by colleagues who choose to look the other way, gossip about the relationship, or lack the skills on how to intervene and confront and help the teacher and student.

In a sense colleagues are also victims. They see the risky behaviors unfolding but do not act. Looking the other way becomes a pattern in a school community that is supposed to be building trust and caring. In the end, as these cases portray, everyone loses: the teacher and student, their families, colleagues, and students who lose trust in the adults in their world; teachers, parents, and community members. Many of these cases could have been prevented with training, supervision, monitoring, and early intervention. The pain that resulted for all involved in these cases didn't have to happen.

The majority of the cases of teacher sexual misconduct involve a relationship between at-risk teachers and needy, at-risk students that emerge out of close contact, often for a prolonged period of time. However, a small number of teachers are predators and use their position of authority to lure vulnerable students into unwanted sexual relationships.

Therefore our training, supervision, monitoring, and intervention efforts need to head off (1) the kinds of budding relationships described in this chapter and (2) the would-be predators described in chapter 4. The good news is that we have developed a beginning profile of educators who have the potential to be at risk of sexual misconduct. The data from these profiles should help us take the necessary next steps in developing training, supervision, monitoring, and intervention programs.

Here is an example of such a profile focusing on teachers who become involved in relationships that lead to sexual misconduct. The majority of teachers involved in sexual misconduct do not go into the profession to prey on students or become involved in inappropriate behavior. They are not predators or psychotics. Sometimes teachers involved in sexual misconduct are star teachers and coaches.

These are professionals who are involved in close contact with students through extracurricular activities and sports. Some are icons whose success as teachers and coaches has earned them a position of power in the school and community, a position that they feel allows them to ignore boundaries, rules, and regulations and become involved in risky behaviors without being detected.

Teachers involved in sexual misconduct tend to justify their behavior by believing that they want their victims to have a deep personal relationship, and sometimes sex, with someone who cares about them. Apparently teachers involved in sexual misconduct easily avoid detection by colleagues and administrators who in fact may be aware of their transgressions but fail to take the necessary steps to intervene to stop the misconduct.

As Lora, a female teacher involved in sexual misconduct in this first case, suggests, "People don't want to see it. The education system doesn't want to talk about this. They want to cover it up."

Many teachers involved in sexual misconduct don't stand out from the crowd and, as Lora suggests, are seemingly normal people who lead normal lives. Often the teacher involved wishes someone had warned him or her early on about the "slippery slope" that can lead to sex with students and that colleagues had warned and confronted them rather than looking the other way or accepting hard to believe cover-ups of their behavior. Colleagues and administrators need to intervene and help when they see teachers like Lora crossing boundaries. Many of the teachers involved and their families experience great shame, guilt, and regret.

There is little sympathy among colleagues for the pain suffered by teachers who cross boundaries, or for their families. There is little awareness that crossing boundaries can happen to any teacher given a combination of personal and professional setbacks. Rather, the teachers are seen as black sheep, out of step, and not representative of the vast majority of trustworthy teachers.

THE CASES OF JOSEPH C. DEBACA AND LORA

This case study puts many of the issues involved in sexual misconduct in perspective and provides us with a beginning road map of how training, supervision, and monitoring can provide early intervention to prevent such behavior. Memories haunt DeBaca[2] as he looks back on his six-year "affair" with a former student that started when she was fourteen: the fear that the police would show up in his classroom to arrest him, the arresting officers who were waiting for him when he returned from a Hawaiian honeymoon, and the visits in jail from his six-year-old daughter.

Also gnawing at him is the thought that all of the anguish could have been avoided if someone had warned him early on about what he terms the "slippery slope" that can lead to sex with students. "What would have really helped me is if someone like myself would have spoken to me when I was a student teacher," said the thirty-seven-year-old former mathematics teacher.

DeBaca and another former Las Vegas teacher convicted of having sex with a student discussed their cases publicly in March 2003 at what was billed as the nation's first conference focused solely on the issue of sexual abuse by school employees. DeBaca and another convicted teacher who appeared at the conference said they had convinced themselves that they were exerting a positive influence in the lives of students with whom they were having sex. "I really wanted her to be with someone who cared about her. That's how I justified it." He said he had no intention of molesting students when he entered teaching.

Both teachers said it was not hard for them to hide what they were doing. "People don't want to see it," said the other former teacher, Lora, a thirty-five-year-old mother. "The education system doesn't want to talk about this. They want to cover it up." Lora said teachers who molest students often don't stand out from the crowd. "If it could happen to someone like me, it could happen to anyone," she said. "We are normal people and we have normal lives."

Warnings from colleagues might have helped her avoid crossing the boundaries into sex with a seventeen-year-old girl she coached in softball at a high school during her first year of teaching. She added, "Teachers have to start opening their eyes and helping each other."

DeBaca, who served a year in prison, said he wanted to speak to future educators to offer his experiences as a cautionary tale. He suggested that educators should become more skeptical of their colleagues. "There were a few educators who said, 'This looks really inappropriate that you're driving her home and spending time with her.' My explanation was her parents wanted me to keep an eye on her," he recalled. "Most teachers said, 'Oh, it's okay if the parents know.' The atmosphere is such that it doesn't stick out when you see a teacher outside the classroom with a student," he added.

DeBaca and Lora say they both suffered great shame and guilt, feelings their families have shared. Both explained that teaching was all they had ever wanted to do and that being barred from the profession was painful for them. However, the participants at the conference, mostly professionals on the front lines of responding to such misconduct, had little sympathy for the pain that the former teachers had caused themselves and their families. The remarks by DeBaca and Lora prompted an angry response from Shannon Knight, a twenty-seven-year-old mother of three from Pahrump, Nevada.

"You guys have no right to classify yourselves as a victim," she said, before getting up and leaving the room in tears. But the heartaches experienced by the students, teachers, and families involved in these episodes can have a positive message for us if we listen to the words of DeBaca and Lora and use their observations to build an effective sexual misconduct intervention.

THE CASE OF GWENDOLYN HAMPTON

Increasingly, reports of sexual misconduct in the schools involve women educators. Of the nearly 250 cases of alleged staff on student sexual misconduct reviewed by *Education Week*, forty-three of them, or nearly one in five, involved female employees. In five of those cases the victims were girls.[3] The rest were boys in middle or high school, ranging in age from eleven to seventeen. Given such a female-dominated profession as education, such numbers evoke little surprise. Therefore in our work to rid the schools of teacher sexual misconduct, we need to raise the awareness that there are women educators who are at risk of sexual misconduct.

For example, thirty-two-year-old Gwendolyn Hampton earned respect as a seemingly devoted Spanish teacher, counselor, houseparent, and single mother at John Dewey Academy, a private boarding school for troubled teenagers in the small western Massachusetts town of Great Barrington.[4] But students and staff at John Dewey said they feel betrayed by Hampton after a federal civil lawsuit alleged that she had a secret sexual relationship with a student, Adam Helfand, and had at least one child by him.

The relationship continued after Helfand graduated from John Dewey and attended college. According to reporter Shelley Murphy, Hampton said, "I didn't believe I did anything wrong. I feel I was good for Adam at the time I had a relationship with him. I certainly wasn't luring or enticing anyone." Helfand, who was expelled from an Illinois high school in 1999 for using drugs and alcohol, was supposed to be getting help for his problems at Dewey. Instead, he said, Hampton gave him alcohol and prescription pills.

The civil suit accuses Hampton of "counseling malpractice." It alleges that Dewey Academy, its president, and its dean were negligent in failing to supervise Hampton. In her defense she said she developed a very close relationship with Helfand because she was asked to do too many things—teach him, serve as his primary counselor, and supervise him when he worked in the school kitchen.

She often called him to her home to babysit or do chores and he became very close to her family. "The boundaries were blurred; I was his lifeline," Hampton said. Even now, Hampton insists she did nothing wrong and cared deeply for Helfand. "I didn't see myself going out with a kid," she said. "I brought out the best in him. He made grown-up decisions, mature decisions."

However, a sense of betrayal is still felt at the school, which is home to twenty-nine high school students, many of whom said their lives have been transformed by the program built on intense confrontational therapy. Matthew, a seventeen-year-old student, credits Hampton's counseling sessions with helping him give up his dishonest and manipulative ways and learn to tell the truth. Diana Gittleman, a lawyer who teaches part time at Dewey

Academy, said that nobody had a clue. "It blows my mind because I think of myself as an intelligent and sophisticated woman," she said.

Hampton's behavior is consistent with our profile. She felt she was good for Adam and was helping him, not trying to date a kid or lure him into a relationship. But as she reports, she became too involved as a teacher, counselor, and supervisor and formed a very close personal relationship with Adam. As the relationship evolved, her own need for such intimate contact emerged, with Adam spending more and more time at her home babysitting and doing chores.

As Murphy reports, Hampton's students were aware of her relationship with Adam. During one of the weekly confrontational group therapy sessions at the school, where staff and students gather in a circle, Hampton acknowledged being questioned about Adam's continuing visits after graduation and whether the relationship was appropriate. She responded, "I said he was having a hard time adjusting to college and I was supportive of him, which was true."

Hampton falls into the category of what researcher and psychologist Jane Kinder Matthews describes as teacher/lovers who fall deeply in love with the teenage student and need frequent validation from others. Matthews supports the major argument in this book when she suggests, "What you have is a needy child and a needy adult and many times, that's just abuse waiting to happen."

THE CASE OF GARY JARVIS

Gary Jarvis provides probably the best example of what can happen when teachers become involved in close personal contact with needy students without adequate training, supervision, monitoring, and intervention. *Newsday* highlighted his abuse in an article titled "School Sex Abuse; Sachem High School Teacher Held in Case Involving Teens."[5] Accounts by community members described him as a model husband and an excellent history teacher at nearby Sachem High School in Ronkonkoma, New York.

But all that changed on June 24, 1996, when Jarvis was arrested for allegedly having sex at a motel with an underage student and fondling a fifteen-year-old student in a classroom. He was arraigned on a third-degree rape charge and a charge of third-degree sexual abuse, both involving students less than sixteen years of age. His neighbors were shocked. This was not the man they knew in the community.

This case prompted me to write a brief *Fastback* on teacher sexual misconduct for Phi Delta Kappa[6] in 1996, in which I briefly described Jarvis's predicament as well as the cases of Glenn Harris, Alois Vlhopolsky, and John Schaenman (also described in this volume).

Jarvis, who was married without children, had been teaching in the Sachem School District for eighteen years. He was successful in the classroom, earned tenure, and had a positive evaluation every year. He had no police record of past sexual misconduct. But as Detective Lieutenant Robert Hoss of the Suffolk County Police Sex Crimes Unit said, "He was taking her to motels for sex. It was more than once or twice, maybe for about a year. He didn't drag her there." Maybe Jarvis "didn't drag her there," but as a professional charged with educating, caring, and protecting his students, he was breaking the law, and the blame ultimately resides with him, not his student, his victim.

School Superintendent James Ruck said that school officials initiated the investigation after a student approached the principal of Sachem High School South. Jarvis was suspended with pay and the police were called in. The teenage girl Jarvis took to motels testified that they had intercourse and oral sex, which Jarvis videotaped and photographed during a ten-month period when she was fifteen and sixteen years old.[7]

On July 18, 1994, Jarvis was sentenced to four to twelve years in prison. According to Smith, before imposing the sentence, Suffolk County Court Judge Kenneth K. Rohl read aloud portions of letters sent to him by a Sachem schoolteacher and the superintendent of Sachem schools, urging prison time for Jarvis and saying his behavior had eroded public esteem for teachers.[8] "He has betrayed a public trust and has victimized young impressionable students," Superintendent Ruck wrote of Jarvis. An unnamed colleague of Jarvis asked the judge to make an example of him, saying, "This may in a small way help to lessen the loss of respect of parents and students for teachers."

Jarvis's behavior should have set off alarms for colleagues, administrators, parents, and community members. But there appears to have been an eerie silence, a pattern of looking the other way, as Jarvis plunged deeper and deeper into sexual misconduct and the margins of school life. Didn't anyone notice? Where were his fellow teachers? It appears there was none of the supervision, monitoring, or intervention that Jarvis needed.

THE CASE OF GLENN HARRIS

It was a high school crush complete with love letters and teddy bears.[9] But it was not the kind of attention any parent would want for a teenage daughter. According to friends, Christina Rosado fell head over heels for her physical education teacher, Glenn Harris, age thirty-three. She was a student at Creative Learning Community, an alternative high school in East Harlem in New York City. Her affection apparently did not go unrequited.

When her mother confronted Christina about the affair in early March, the girl and Harris disappeared together on a countrywide tour of cheap motels and amusement parks, stopping to inquire about marriage laws. Harris was charged with kidnapping. After a nationwide hunt for Harris and Christina, Harris surrendered to Edward Stancik, the special commissioner for investigations for New York City schools on May 16, 1995.[10]

Harris's case presented an opportunity to turn a spotlight on the ugly and mostly hidden problem of contact between school staff members and students.[11] Edward Stancik said, "I don't want people to think there are massive hordes of child molesters in the school but it is certainly true that there are lots of relationships betweens adolescents and school staff."

People in the system need to blow a very loud whistle when they become aware of sexual contact between an employee and a student. Harris came into the teaching profession with known problems. According to reporter Russ Buettner, Harris was a former police officer who was asked to quit because of "attitudinal problems." He was a first-year teacher, beginning in September 1994, with no training or experience in working with needy adolescents in an alternative school environment.

As the teaching year progressed, Harris ignored boundaries by making romantic gestures toward Christina during school hours, taking her out to lunch and dinner, giving her gifts, and exchanging love letters and notes. This behavior was ignored by colleagues and school administrators. Harris fit the profile of a teacher headed toward sexual misconduct without the necessary training, supervision, monitoring, and intervention, for the following reasons.[12]

Harris was often seen talking alone with the girl with the classroom door closed, strolling with her in Central Park, and asking her out for dinner. Although Harris's actions toward students raised some suspicions, other colleagues and students described him as attractive and trustworthy. He was "not a guy you'd watch out for," a school official said. "This is a guy everyone trusted."

No formal complaint was lodged by the school until January, when Harris was transferred to Landmark School for "unrelated reasons." Evidence of the relation came on March 7, when the girl's mother intercepted a letter her daughter had sent to Harris that was returned for insufficient postage. The letter clearly showed that the two were lovers.

After Harris fled with Christina, her girlfriends at school did not seem to be worried about her. "A lot of people in the class just think they ran away together," said Takiyah Tinsley, age fourteen. "They thought they were going out together."

The Creative Learning Community, a school for underachieving or high-risk children, encourages friendships between students and teachers, teachers said, but it was clear to them that Harris, who was fresh out of graduate school, was crossing the bounds of propriety.

When Harris surrendered to police on May 16, 1995, he justified his actions by painting himself as Rosado's savior. Harris said, "A student came to me with horrific tales of brutal family abuse that lasted years and years. Whatever happens, I hope someone steps in. She is a beautiful person and deserves respect."

The administration failed to intervene. Administrators failed to provide the necessary safety and protection for Christina and intervention for Harris.

Marginal students, like Christina Rosado, and their parents deserve better. They don't deserve to come into a new school that offers hope and opportunity and find themselves instead involved with at-risk, untrained teachers who have no idea how to establish professional boundaries and keep their personal needs separate. And they don't deserve the kind of school in which administrators fail to look out for their welfare and quickly address a teacher on the way to trouble.

THE CASE OF DR. D/ALOIS DLHOPOLSKY

Alois Dlhopolsky was known as "Dr. D" at Holy Trinity High School in Hicksville, New York. The science teacher spent extra time with students if they needed help with physics or chemistry and was a teacher they would talk to about personal problems.[13] When a sixteen-year-old student had trouble with her boyfriend and her parents at the end of 1991, she turned to Dr. D for guidance. By May 1992, he was calling her at home and a month later they started "hanging out in school together" and he would drive her to his home in nearby Lindenhurst. There, according to reporter Michele Salcedo, they had sex.

But it wasn't until three years later that the former student, now nineteen, came forward to report the encounter to police. Dlhopolsky was fired from the school in February 1996 and charged with statutory rape; he maintained his innocence. According to his lawyer, Joseph Caramagno, Dlhopolsky "apparently had known the girl for a period of time. He maintained a friendship with her after she graduated. He denies any sexual involvement. It's the kind of thing that could happen to any teacher. I guess his mistake was being friends with her at all."

However, Drew Biondo, the district attorney, said there was nothing in the investigation to indicate the young woman had any reason to come forward other than the fact that she believed she had been wronged. In her statement to the police, the young woman said, "I always felt what happened was wrong and that if I didn't have the problems to talk to Dr. D about this wouldn't happen. I started thinking if this was my kid, this wouldn't be right."

But according to Salcedo, other students were angry that the school fired Dr. D simply on an accusation. One student, Dale Thomas, said, "Everybody knows she would go there for extra help. Dr. D was a great guy. He'd come to our plays; he'd come to sports night. He never propositioned anybody, he never came on or anything like that." In February 1996, Dlhopolsky accepted a plea bargain.[14]

Caramagno suggested that his mistake "was being friends with her at all." As student Dale Thomas said, "Everybody knows she would go to his room for extra help." Remember the words of Dr. Ava L. Siegler, director of the Institute for Child, Adolescent, and Family Studies in New York City, that any adolescent is vulnerable; they are all looking for someone to emulate and offer approval.[15] She says, "Yet psychologically, they may not be ready to deal with the consequences of physical and emotional intimacy."

KELLY ANNE GALLIGAN

In reviewing cases of teacher sexual misconduct, I have found two themes that play a predominant role in almost every case, whether it involves a relationship between an at-risk teacher and a needy student or a predator teacher luring a student into unwanted sex. One overriding theme is the lack of supervision, monitoring, and accountability of teachers involved in such inappropriate behaviors. The other is the lack of intervention even when crossing boundaries and being too involved in close relationships with students is beyond question.

Kelly Anne Galligan, a teacher in Lisbon Falls, Maine, was accused of having sexual relations with a student she was tutoring. As reported by the Associated Press in March 1995, Galligan, a third-grade teacher, had sex with a fourteen-year-old student she was tutoring "on a pretty regular basis" during the fall of 1993.[16] The boy said he "didn't think it was such a big deal" and that the sexual encounters took place in Galligan's apartment in a house she was watching for its owner and at the student's home while his mother and younger sisters were asleep in their upstairs bedrooms.

Galligan was indicted in December 1993 of having sexual relations with this boy and another teenager half her age. She was forced to resign from her teaching position. How did such a vivid tale of a teacher's crossing boundaries and ignoring the red light of danger evolve? At her trial, Galligan was described by her lawyer as a dedicated teacher who believed her job didn't end when she left the classroom.

She spent many nonteaching hours tutoring students and helping steer them away from drugs. But clearly that prolonged time with students was risky for Galligan as well. The victim indicated Galligan bought him dinner at "nice restaurants," took him shopping for back-to-school clothes, and helped him with book reports and math homework. Gilligan was seen in restaurants with the boy, in stores buying him clothes, and was known to be meeting with him in her home and his home to help with reports and homework, get-togethers that, as the boy said, "usually involved having sex."

Galligan even allowed the boy to bring his friends to her apartment while they were high on marijuana and stay the night. In the end her behavior was finally noticed. Rumors began to circulate throughout the town that Galligan was having sex with teenage boys, rumors that prompted police to conduct a surveillance of her apartment.

As Deputy District Attorney Craig Turner suggested at the trial, "What had been a friendship developed into a romantic relationship." Nowhere in the Associated Press article is there any mention of involvement by school officials.

On December 13, 1994, a judge ruled that the evidence presented by the prosecution that Galligan had made self-incriminating statements could not be used because a Lisbon Falls police detective who was a friend had tricked her into making the statements.[17] So while Galligan admitted the relationship on March 11, 1995, she was acquitted of the charge of sexual abuse.[18] Galligan's lawyer, Leonard Sharon, focused on a civil suit the parents of the boy had brought against Galligan, telling the jurors, "It sounds like it's about money to me." But the alleged behaviors didn't go away and Galligan lost her teaching job, her career, and her reputation.

NOTES

1. Roberta G. Simmons and Dale A. Blyth, *Moving into Adolescence: The Impact of Puberty Changes and School Context* (New York: Aldine De Gruyter, 1987), xii, 304, 351–52.

2. Caroline Hendrie, "Experts Convene on Sexual Abuse by Teachers," *Education Week*, April 9, 2003, http://www.edweek.org/ew/ewstory/cfm?slug=30abuse.h22.

3. Caroline Hendrie, "Abuse by Women Raises Its Own Set of Problems," *Education Week*, December 2, 1998, http://www.edweek.org/ew/vol-18/14women.h18.

4. Shelley Murphy, "Teacher in Abuse Suit Defends Actions," *Boston*, September 14, 2004, http://www.boston.com/news/local/articles/2004/09/14/teacher_in_abuse_suit_defends _act.

5. Ellen Yan and Robin Topping, "School Sex Abuse: Sachem H.S. Teacher Held in Case Involving Teen," *Newsday*, June 25, 1993, 3 (A).

6. William L. Fibkins, *Preventing Teacher Sexual Misconduct* (Bloomington, IN: Phi Delta Kappa Education Foundation, 1996), 11–15.

7. Estelle Lander Smith, "Teen to Testify at Teacher Sex Trial," *Newsday*, May 6, 1994, 25 (A).

8. Estelle Lander Smith, "Jail for Teacher in Student's Sex Abuse," *Newsday*, July 19, 1994, 4 (A).

9. Russ Buettner, "Teacher, Teen on the Run for Love," *Newsday*, May 11, 1995, 6 (A).

10. Carey Goldberg, "Manhattan Teacher Surrenders in Kidnapping of Teenage Girl," *New York Times*, May 17, 1995, 1 (A), 4 (B).

11. Bob Herbert, "An Ugly School Situation," *New York Times*, May 17, 1995, 19 (A).

12. Carey Goldberg, "Nationwide Hunt for Teacher and Girl, 15," *New York Times*, May 11, 1995, 1, 8 (B).

13. Michele Salcedo, "Teacher in Rape Case Popular in School," *Newsday*, February 22, 1995, 7 (A).

14. Geoffrey Mohan, "Guilty in Teen Sex," *Newsday*, February 22, 1997, 27 (A).

15. Margot Slade, "Yes, Statutory Rape Is Still a Rather Big Deal," *New York Times*, June 11, 1995, 9 (E).

16. Associated Press, "Maine Teen-ager Testifies of Sex with Ex-teacher," *Boston Globe*, March 9, 1995, 26.

17. Associated Press, "Evidence against Teacher Barred," *Boston*, October 13, 1994, http://nl.newsbank.com/nl-search/we/Archives?p_action=print.

18. Associated Press, "Maine Third-Grade Teacher Acquitted of Sexually Abusing Two Teen-Age Boys," *Boston Globe*, March 11, 1995, 14 (Metro).

Chapter Three

Cases of Coaches Who Become Involved in Sexual Misconduct

Chapter 3 will focus on cases that illuminate the risks involved in long-term, intensive, and close relations between educators and students, such as the kind that can develop when male faculty members coach female athletes. These cases provide a classic example of the mischief that can happen concerning the impact of the early 1970s Title IX legislation, which spawned a wave of new sports teams for young women.

These sports teams were often coached by male faculty members who had no training in how to carry on close contact with young women, many of whom saw their coaches as adult role models and the key to athletic scholarships and admissions to prized colleges and universities.[1]

However, school leaders and parents never saw the risks involved for students until cases of sexual misconduct began to emerge, often with the victims being vilified and accused of a vendetta against successful, politically connected coaches who were community icons. Putting together a profile of coaches who become involved in sexual misconduct is not difficult. In many of these cases, there are clear signals that coaches were crossing boundaries.

Yet as is often the case in sexual misconduct and a key lesson in this book, in almost every case administrators, colleagues, parents, and peers failed to help the victims involved. Here is a tentative profile of coaches who are at risk for sexual misconduct.

Many coaches are community icons. Their winning records make them a resource for the school district's positive public relations for the school and community's pride, often in a time of calls for budget cuts.

Because of their iconic status, coaches tend to be politically connected. They bring winning teams to the community, putting the community and its schools on the front page of area newspapers and television stations, increasing scholarships and college admissions for student athletes, and serving as a draw to bring new parents and their athletic children into the community all tend to provide the coaches with star status.

As such, they are often beyond reproach and not required to follow the same rules and boundaries as other educators. As these case studies suggest, they are their own bosses and supervisors. They are free to roam and act as they choose in their school and community, a dangerous mix.

As male faculty members, they have had little or no training in how to coach and carry on close contact with female athletes over a long period of time. The advent of Title IX not only created many new coaching opportunities with female athletes, but also presented the inevitable abuse waiting to happen.

As in other cases of sexual misconduct, many of the victims of coaches' sexual misconduct are afraid to report the incidents to school officials or their parents. They tend to feel that they need the coaches' support to gain admission to colleges and scholarship aid. This is particularly true for impoverished students who lack resources to support a college education.

In a real sense, many of these students are victims, trapped between either going along with their coaches' sexual advances or risking the loss of their support if they failed to go along and go as far as to report their sexual advances to the proper authorities.

Plus the victims and their parents who come forward are often vilified and accused of waging a vendetta or trying to ruin the professional careers and personal lives of dedicated educators. In some cases, they also experience threats to stop the accusations. The lesson? We don't want to hear any more talk about sexual misconduct on the part of our coaches.

THE CASE OF JOE SUTTON

Many cases of sexual relations between educators and vulnerable students involve educators who lead extracurricular activities, such as coaches. Male coaches involved with high school female athletes stand out as a particularly risky environment for both coaches and students. But we should not be surprised by this phenomenon. The Title IX law enacted in 1972 barring sexual discrimination in schools that receive federal money opened the gates for young women to participate in organized athletics.

Participation in women's athletic teams rocketed from 300,000 to 3 million in the wake of Title IX, creating a need for thousands of new coaches, many of them men who had little or no training in how to work in close, prolonged contact with female students who often saw these male coaches as mentors to help them obtain scholarships and admission to select colleges and universities.[2] Some of these female athletes were clearly manipulated, even forced, to "go along" with a coach's sexual advances because they believed they needed their help to win a college scholarship. Many were trapped in what they saw as a no-win situation with no adult intervention available to help them out of a conflict not of their own doing.

Therefore, in my view, the attempt of Title IX to solve a problem created a problem. In the effort to create women's teams in basketball, lacrosse, softball, tennis, track, volleyball, soccer, and badminton, the pattern in many schools was to hire male coaches who were already on staff coaching football, baseball, soccer, and basketball with little or no training or orientation, announce that a program for female students was in place, and let the games begin. In a sense the male coaches, already bonded and members of the school's coaching fraternity, took over the emerging women's athletic program, seeing it as an opportunity to expand their career opportunities, but had little preparation for the new personal and professional dynamics they would face.

Don Sabo, a sociology professor at D'Youville College in Buffalo, New York, attributes the predominance of male coaches in the wake of Title IX to various factors, including an upswing in male applicants for jobs that did not previously exist or did not pay as well as they did now, and a bias by some male athletic directors against hiring female candidates. In today's high school athletic programs, men coach the majority of women's teams.

But there is a dark side to the male dominance of women's athletic teams. In the wake of Title IX, what really happened was that school officials and athletic directors planted the seeds for sexual misconduct. School officials and athletic directors failed to consider the human aspects of male coaches, many of them in the twenty- to thirty-year-old age category, becoming involved with adolescents who were beginning to explore their own sexuality.

For example, before the public congratulations after games escalated to private embraces in a schoolroom, Amanda Henderson said she found it flattering that a veteran high school football coach would take such an uncommon interest in her, a sophomore basketball player. Henderson recalled that the coach, Joe Sutton, refused to let anyone else tape her ankles before her games at Indian Land High School in North Carolina and, to the vexation of her female basketball coach, did not want anyone else around when he taped them.

He never missed Henderson's games, chose Henderson as his student aide, and showered her with gifts like the basketball T-shirts she collected. During softball season, when he served as assistant coach, he parked himself at third base, her position, and supervised her every move. Henderson thought he wanted her to be a winner.

But, she said, he gradually began to demand a dividend for his devotion. The hugs and compliments were followed by invitations to spend time with

Sutton away from school. Henderson's parents became suspicious and eventually mobilized a school board investigation that resulted in Sutton's resignation in January 1998.

It was not a pretty picture for Amanda. But again, we should not be surprised. Don Sabo suggests there is a special relationship between athlete and coach and "it's all about emotions, about trust and about the body. And when scholarships come into play, it's about money, too." However, in my opinion, it can also be all about using one's position of authority as a coach to manipulate a young student into being his victim. Joe Sutton went to great lengths to create a web that made it difficult for Amanda to see his real intentions. She thought she was in good hands, safe, until Sutton's real intentions became clear.

Clearly there is more opportunity for female athletes than ever before, but the flip side is that there is more risk to athletes because we haven't developed effective training, supervision, monitoring, and intervention programs that would have enabled school officials, the athletic director, fellow coaches, and colleagues to quickly intervene to stop Joe Sutton before he proceeded to cross boundaries.

Dr. Joel Fish, director of the Center for Sports Psychology in Philadelphia, observes, "When you put a male into a position of power where he can manipulate something of real meaning to an athlete, such as playing time or scholarships, then add in the possibility of a young girl who may have a crush, you've got an extremely dangerous mix." Sutton's connection to Henderson had destructive consequences for her. Henderson, accused of exaggerating Sutton's overtures, was ostracized by her teammates. The school board investigation of Sutton turned up complaints that he had committed indiscretions with at least four other students.

THE CASE OF RICK LOPEZ

Sexual misconduct doesn't just happen. As the case studies in this book demonstrate, sexual misconduct most often occurs in an environment that allows professional caregivers such as teachers and coaches to operate on their own, without guidelines, clear boundaries, training, supervision, and intervention. Often those in positions of authority, whether they are administrators, teachers, parents, or community leaders, don't take notice or, when alerted to possible sexual misconduct, turn the other way. The turning away process is not always intentional and clear-cut. Rather, the process of choosing not to speak out and confront sexual misconduct is subtler and more confusing for the observer.

As shown in many of these case studies, otherwise concerned professionals, parents, and citizens often mistrust their own initial observations and reactions; they feel that this kind of behavior can't be happening in their school, community, and before their own eyes. They may have long-term relationships and allegiances with the professional involved and they may lack the skills and sometimes the courage to confront such behavior.

Clearly Title IX, with all its good intentions, provided fertile territory for sexual misconduct to take place and allowed other adults to avoid the necessary intervention. The checks and balances to prevent misconduct were not in place in many schools. Untrained coaches were suddenly thrown together with aspiring female athletes who saw the coaches as their tickets to stardom.

The male coaches described in this chapter are not predators. They were male teachers following the same script they used for male athletes. What they didn't foresee was the possibility of physical and emotional attraction with these female student athletes, nor did they have the skills in how to set in place boundaries that might serve to protect their students from abuse and harmful sexual relationships. Coaching female athletes was different and required a different script.

Title IX opened up a broad frontier for secondary school and college female athletes. Junior and senior high schools throughout the United States began fielding teams in basketball, soccer, volleyball, tennis, softball, gymnastics, golf, field hockey, and badminton. Often the coaches hired were males who already served as coaches for male teams. They knew the school system and the bureaucracy, had experience as winning coaches, and knew the ins and outs of helping their athletes gain admission and scholarships to major college and university athletic programs.

Many coaches used their positions of power to become politically connected with influential community members through the use of booster clubs that financed parts of the athletic programs that lacked funding, such as new stadiums, uniforms, trips, publicity, and so forth. Their role and position of power was akin to a small-town mayor. Doors closed to others were open to them and their athletes. They were stars in their own right, a "somebody" as the saying goes.

These winning and politically savvy coaches understood that an important part of their job was to create the same liaisons with college coaches that they had made with their male students; that is, to literally sell their newly developed women's programs and student athletes to the highest bidder—colleges and universities that could offer the best scholarships and playing opportunities and be a springboard to life as a professional player in sports like basketball, soccer, and tennis.

Many coaches understood that in addition to coaching, this kind of "selling" was the key to continuing their position of power in the school and community. The bottom line was that the community respected not only the number of games and championships won on the playing field, but also the number of female athletes winning scholarships and prized college admissions. The bigger the numbers, the more secure their position.

They knew that their survival depended on greasing the relationship between the school and college admission officers, coaches, and travel team and summer tourney guru coaches. Coaching was just one part of their powerful position. Successfully selling their products to the highest bidder was as important. The tremendous rise in women's basketball at the high school and college level became the major vehicle for showcasing the emerging female stars, stars who would go on to fill the collegiate ranks.

They showcased their talented female athletes by establishing a liaison between their star athletes and the so-called traveling teams or clubs that play on after the regular school season, local, state, and even national club leagues and tournaments, and at the growing number of year-round camps and workshops led by coaching gurus with a national reputation who acted as headhunters on the lookout for players with the potential to star at the college level. For some gifted high school athletes the season never ended. It was no longer about girls having fun playing high school ball.

It became a year-long process that involved constant practicing, playing, doing well, getting noticed, getting one's name in the paper, and being helped to create a polished, professional-sounding résumé and videotape that could be forwarded to any interested coach.

Yes, many parents were heavily involved, giving up their own personal lives and resources to make sure their aspiring athletic children had access to tournaments, camps, and workshops, settings that offered the best hope of landing a spot with a Division I team, which represented the highest achievement for many student athletes. But in the process, many parents found they were giving up more than time, resources, and unconditional support.

If their student athlete was gifted, they often found that the gurus who coached and administered the traveling teams, tournaments, and camps would begin slowly but firmly to take over the lives of their children. The coaches demanded that the parents let the child spend more and more time with them so they could compete for scholarships, college admissions, and notoriety.

The coaches also encouraged their student athletes to abandon the social aspects of high school life and involvement with peers. In a sense it was an informal contract between the guru coach and the parent and child, a contract that suggested, "If you want to get ahead and get to Division I, you do what I say. I am in charge, not you or your parents. I'll do all the thinking. Your job is to listen to me. I'll show you how to get better and get to where you've always dreamed of being. The crowds, the notoriety, the scholarships are there. Listen to me and me alone. The days of high school fun are over. This is work and serious business."

So as the dark side of Title IX ran its course, many young women abandoned their friends, their teenage lives, the fun part of sports, and even their parents. They joined a select group of other female athletes in a cult-like environment led by the guru coach. It was a family whose sole purpose was to outperform others. They became like their gifted male counterparts, always future oriented, preparing and learning how to sell themselves to the highest bidder.

The fun days were over. What are those summer camps and tourneys like for high school students who are college hopefuls? Dozens of college coaches were seated courtside during a July 2003 game between the Colorado Hoopsters and the Minnesota Metro Stars at the Clackamas Community College gym in Oregon City, Oregon.[3]

The coaches present represented colleges and universities from some of the biggest names in women's basketball. Winter recruiting helps, but coaches wanting to take their teams deep into National Collegiate Athletic Association (NCAA) tournaments needed to get top players seen, not heard, in gyms such as this one. Notre Dame's Muffet McGraw and Stanford's Tara Van Derveer joined Colorado's Ceal Berry and Chris Denker of Colorado State on the two rows, one at each end of the court.

They were separated from the rest of the crowd because NCAA rules forbid contact between college coaches and the girls' summer club coaches. There were also coaches from other schools such as Dartmouth, Xavier, Lafayette, Maryland, and Vanderbilt. Many of the coaches start their summer recruiting here with four hundred coaches watching 159 teams. The girls' summer circuit is booming. The tournament started in 1979 with eight teams.

Maryland coach Brenda Frese calls this kind of summer tournament "one hundred times better" than what she sees watching high school teams in the winter. "High school? Ugh. I can't even stand to watch high school ball to be honest. It's not the same level. It's not the same intensity. A majority of these summer players have a level where they can play whether it's Division I, II, or III."

But these summer tourneys have pitfalls for high school athletes. Bill Saum, the NCAA's director of agent, gambling, and amateur activities, suggests that there is almost no oversight compared to high school basketball. "The goal here is to encourage the recruiting process to be moved into the high school, so our coaches can deal with the high school coaches, high school administrators, and the families of the players. These people clearly have the best interest of the student-athlete in mind. It's an academically based environment. They're around these kids for reasons more than basketball."

But the reality is that the college coaches profit from these summer tourneys, which allow them to see a large number of players in a short time. And that is not about to change. The gurus, like Rick Lopez, who coached the

Colorado Hoopsters until 2003, will remain powerful figures in the lives of aspiring women basketball hopefuls.

Rick Lopez and his Colorado Hoopsters gained national prominence as a basketball training program that could pretty much guarantee any woman basketball player automatic access to a college scholarship and stardom. That is, until Lopez was charged with having ongoing sexual relationships with some of his players and committed suicide on December 26, 2004, at 12:22 a.m.

Upon reflection, many parents admitted to being lured into the program with the promises of a college scholarship but once inside the Hoopsters "family" they witnessed the dark side—the punishments, the paybacks, and the atmosphere of fear that they say coach Rick Lopez used to control every corner of his program. That culture was further tainted by allegations of sexual contact between Lopez and some players, yet few families ever walked away from the elite program.

As we all know, when we allow ourselves, our families, or our children to be abused by others without raising an alarm, confronting the problem, or simply walking away, that signals the Rick Lopezs of the world to take even more freedoms because they know they will not be challenged. They are in the driver's seat and calling out the orders. The student athletes and their parents become the followers. Lopez upped the ante with his star players. Once he had complete control over the players and reduced their parents to observer status, Lopez moved into new territory—sexual relationships with some of his players.

At first he denied any such conduct and called the rumors attacks on the Hoopsters program. Then, in 2003, three ex-Hoopsters accused Lopez of having or trying to have sexual contact with them and a fourth said she witnessed him having inappropriate contact with another player.[4] The players were eighteen years of age or younger at the time of the incidents.

Lopez denied all the charges but admitted to spending the night at some players' homes. He said his stays were never improper and the players' parents always welcomed him. Lopez said his close friendships with several girls and their families fueled years of false perceptions and jealous rumors by other Hoopster parents and opposing coaches.

In the mid-1990s, the Boulder County Sheriff's Office investigated Lopez's association with the then-fifteen-year-old who has since talked to the *Denver Post*. At that time she told detectives she had no contact with the coach. No charges were filed. Several years later, an anonymous caller contacted the Highland Ranch Middle School, where the Hoopsters practice, and raised concerns about the coach.

The school administration looked into those concerns but found no reason to change their rental agreement with Lopez. In the summer of 2003, the Douglas County Sheriff's Office interviewed Hoopster parents, current players, and former players about Lopez but reported that they had "no credible evidence at this point." In the summer of 2003, Lopez was still supported by many parents who discounted the rumors as gossip.

"Parents make up stories and it's pure downright jealousy," said Barbara Walters, whose daughter Keirsten starred for the Hoopsters in the mid-1990s and later played at the University of Connecticut. Lopez continued to accuse opposing coaches of generating sexual innuendo about him as a ploy to shut down his program and steal his players.

He suggested that the rumors about him had circulated so long that some people started believing them. However, he indicated that "maybe it's time for me to move on." The *Denver Post* ran a series about Lopez in October 2003 that included allegations of possible sexual misconduct. He remained with the team until July 30, 2004, when he abruptly left the team in the middle of a tournament in Oregon. On July 30, 2004, Lopez was arrested and charged with fifty-five felony sexual assault charges and four misdemeanor charges for having sex with three players who were minors.[5]

He committed suicide on December 26, 2004, by hanging. Lopez had threatened suicide in tapes made in July 2004 of phone calls between him and one of the players he allegedly assaulted. He also apologized to one girl on the tape about the alleged incidents. Chris Denker, head women's basketball coach at Colorado State, where several former Hoopsters have played, called the apparent suicide Lopez's final crime and said it robbed ex-Hoopsters and victims of a choice to heal through the legal process.

There are many lessons to be learned from the Rick Lopez case and the saga of the Colorado Hoopsters. Here are some examples.

We need to educate professional staff members—teachers and coaches— parents, and students to beware of gurus and saviors who promise fame and fortune but have their own personal agendas. They need to recognize the danger amid the glory involved in sports.

We need to create school environments that offer ongoing training, supervision, and intervention to teachers and coaches involved in long-term close contact with students, particularly male coaches with female students.

We need to create a school and community-wide helping network in which professional staff, students, parents, and community members are alert to possible sexual misconduct and are encouraged to act and not freeze.

We need to closely examine student, parent, and professional staff relationships with organizations outside the school that may damage students.

We need to teach our students that walking away from a hurtful and perhaps destructive situation, albeit sponsored with good intentions, is an appropriate choice.

We need to teach our students, parents, professional staff, and community leaders that there can be a downside to excelling in sports.

We need to raise the awareness of school district leaders—superintendents, principals, athletic directors, coaches, guidance counselors, and PTA presidents—that it can be harmful to use gifted athletes as merchandise and public relations tools to sell their communities and colleges and universities on the success of their programs and promote both the athlete's and district's success by encouraging participation in unregulated and unsupervised out-of-school programs over which the district has no control.

Finally, as the NCAA's Bill Saum suggests, we need to advocate a recruiting process for student athletes that is "led by high school coaches, administrators, and families. Those people who clearly have the best interest of the student athletes in mind. They're around these kids for reasons more than basketball."

THE CASE OF THE SOUTHINGTON HIGH SCHOOL GIRLS' BASKETBALL AND SOFTBALL COACHES

As we see in some school settings, there is a climate that turns a blind eye to sexual misconduct by a group of teachers and coaches in spite of ongoing rumors of such behaviors in the school community. These are school settings in which a powerful group of educators has taken over and been given free rein to prey on vulnerable students without fear of detection. It appears such was the case at Southington High School dating from the late 1970s through the late 1980s.

Southington, Connecticut, is a picturesque New England community located twenty miles from Hartford, the state capital. The town has many churches and civic groups. In the 1970s and 1980s, the high school had approximately 1,700 students in grades nine through twelve. The community had a great interest in the schools and successful athletic programs, including the emerging interest in girls' sports at the high school level that began in the mid-1970s. For many in Southington, this was the best of times for girls' high school sports.[6]

Southington High School's 1981–1982 girls' basketball team captured the school's first girls' basketball championship under coach Joseph C. Daddio. The same year, the girls' softball team, led by Coach Joseph J. Piazza, won its fourth state championship in five years. The girls' teams were a community treasure. Their victories were the talk of street corners, bars, and beauty salons, and their back-to-back championships catapulted the already popular coaches and their teams to new levels of prominence.

The success of Southington High's girls' teams was well publicized and the players were devoted to the male coaches who brought them that fame. However, twenty years later the public would learn that there was a seamier side to the girls' sports teams.

At least a dozen former players from that period have told police that Daddio, Piazza, and some former assistant coaches, including Raymond Acey, Bob Shirley, and teacher William McKernan, had sex with them and others or made inappropriate sexual overtures or both. The popular coaches and teacher were all married and in their late twenties or early thirties at the time the incidents allegedly occurred.

"These guys were famous in town," said a former basketball player, who added that her relationship with one of the assistant coaches in the late 1970s involved kissing and petting. "Everyone was thrilled that our girls' teams were winning. The feeling was that the coaches couldn't do anything wrong. You'd never think of challenging them on how they behaved."

Another woman who claimed she had a sexual relationship with Daddio in the mid-1980s said, "At the time I thought the attention was a good thing because I thought it meant the coach had noticed me and it would benefit the team." And as one woman who played softball and basketball in the early 1980s and said she had a sexual relationship with Acey observed, "We grew up watching the Southington High School teams before us win state championships and we dreamed of having the same opportunities. Girls did not have the opportunities they have now. Times were different. A coach making a pass at you was not something you told anyone about."

How did a group of girls' basketball and softball coaches become involved in sexual relationships with their players in such a close-knit community for such a long period of time without intervention? This was not a case of one coach acting as a predator. There were five coaches involved. And these five coaches used a variety of threats to keep their victims silenced, threats that appear to have worked for many years. Two former Southington High School female basketball players talked of losing their virginity to coaches, while other female athletes described coaches making sexually tinged comments, rubbing their legs, and kissing them.[7]

They told police that the coaches took advantage of their positions as trusted mentors to pursue sexual relationships. Those are among the allegations of misconduct involving several high school coaches and more than a dozen female athletes from the mid-1970s through the 1980s that were described in a police report released in early January of 2002.

The men accused were former high school teacher and girls' basketball coach Joseph Daddio; former middle school teacher and assistant basketball coach Raymond Acey; high school math teacher, softball coach, and former assistant high school basketball coach Joseph Piazza; middle school science teacher William McKernan; and former assistant basketball coach Robert Shirley. All denied any wrongdoing except Shirley, who could not be located.

The police report summarized an investigation launched in October 2000 that was prompted by a complaint from a woman who did not want her niece in a class with Daddio. The woman told police that about twenty years earlier she had sexual relations with Daddio in his home, her home, and a local motel. Daddio submitted his resignation as a business education teacher on October 13, 2000, after the former student came forward. He was accused of having sexual relations with two students and engaging in inappropriate behavior and contact with at least two others.

Acey resigned the following month after similar allegations against him surfaced. He was accused of having sexual relations with two students, making sexual comments to another student while he was her coach and later, after she graduated, developing a sexual relationship with her, and counseling many girls in his locked classroom. Piazza was placed on administrative leave following release of the report. He was accused of having a sexual relationship with a former student that started several weeks after she graduated, having a sexual relationship with another student, touching one student in an inappropriate manner, and having inappropriate contact with players.

During the police investigation, a number of women came forward, many saying they knew their basketball and softball teammates were having sex with coaches and some coaches, including Piazza, had intimate relationships with multiple students. Shirley, a volunteer assistant coach, was accused of having a sexual relationship with a student during her junior year. The police report indicated that he provided alcohol for her and let her stay overnight at his apartment.

As part of the police investigation, one woman described herself as Shirley's "project." She was sixteen and Shirley was thirty when she lost her virginity to him. Afterward Shirley told her that she would be "blackballed" from colleges she wanted to attend if she ever told anyone about their relationship.

Shirley's whereabouts remain unknown. McKernan was accused of kissing an eighth-grade basketball player on the lips several times at after-school events and telling her that he would kiss her for every block she made on the court. The team's three female chaperones accused McKernan of touching players during basketball drills and telling them how romantic he was. He was placed on paid leave in January 2004 but returned to teaching and coaching with only a reprimand. School officials defended their handling of the 2002 complaint against McKernan, saying the evidence wasn't strong enough.[8]

However, as in many other cases of sexual misconduct, the reaction of the community was split. Residents and former players rushed to defend the coaches, blitzing local newspapers with letters to the editor and questioning the validity of the women's complaints.

One former player who came forward said, "Instead of the community jumping to the support of victims, they have gone straight to asking these former female student athletes why they waited twenty-plus years to tell their stories; why don't they ask the teachers and coaches why they have not yet come forward to confess their sins?"

A January 14, 2002, *New York Times* article titled "Town's Disgust Outlasts a Statute of Limitation" reported that in the aftermath of the police report released on January 8, 2002, there was a high level of disgust in Southington, particularly that the coaches involved could not be charged because the statute of limitations for prosecuting such contact is seven years.[9]

There was also hostile reaction by some community members to the news that William McKernan was simply reprimanded and allowed to stay in the classroom and resume his coaching duties. As the *Times* reported, George DiBattista, who had lived in the town for thirty years, said, "No one should get away with that and these guys are still getting a pension and everything."

Matthew Welinsky, whose daughter was a student at Southington High during the 1980s, said, "It's a black eye on the face of the town. You think you can trust teachers and that your children are safe and then you hear about something like this going on without anyone knowing it." An editorial in the *Hartford Courant* on June 4, 2004, echoes the community disgust by stating that Mr. McKernan should have been removed from coaching, given the complaint and the ample evidence of a culture of permissiveness in the athletic department. "A virus isn't curable but it should be contained."

There are many lessons in the Southington case. Here are some examples.

1. Coaches who have outstanding athletic teams can slip into sexual misconduct with their team members. They have been promoted to a place of prominence in the community and feel they have no limits or boundaries. Absent training, supervision, monitoring, and intervention, successful coaches can become renegades preying on innocent victims.

2. Many adults in leadership roles in the school surprisingly state they had no indication of the sexual misconduct of the coaches. School officials during the time of the alleged incidents admit to being equally surprised by the allegations, insisting they saw no hints that anything was wrong. "Absolutely not, I never knew anything about it, and if I had, I would have done something," said David Larson, a former assistant superintendent. Former athletic director Dominic D'Angelo also said, "Absolutely not. I never heard of any reports of any misconduct on the part of coaches. I had never had a complaint." Corine Lorenzet, who headed the high school guidance department, had no comment.

In the police report, one woman said she told Lorenzet just a few years ago about a sexual relationship between Daddio and her sister. The woman told Lorenzet about the relationship because she wanted her son removed from Daddio's class. According to the report, the student was removed from Daddio's class but the allegations were never investigated. Someone with authority had to have known. As parent Sharon Dinsmore, who had two daughters who played high school basketball in the 1980s, said, "There were rumors around. I certainly heard them. I believe a lot of people were aware of the possibility of impropriety and didn't pursue it."

3. Close contact between coaches and players that lasts over long periods of time can be risky when coaches are not trained in how to carry on such behaviors without crossing boundaries. Clearly no red light went off for Daddio, Piazza, and the other coaches.

4. High school athletes who are victims of sexual misconduct may be threatened into holding their silence because of their need for recommendations for college scholarships from the same coaches and teachers who are abusing them. As one former student said, "I needed to play ball. I wanted to get some scholarship help because I knew my parents couldn't afford to send me to school for four years. I went along with the relationship." The increased pressure on high school students to get a leg up on admissions to colleges and secure scholarships may act to silence students who are victims of sexual misconduct. They may "go along," naïvely trusting that the abuse they are enduring will have a happy ending, buoyed by the words of coaches and teachers who promise scholarships and early admissions.

5. The coaches involved focused on players with parents who were either inattentive to their comings and goings or, like most, believed their daughters were in caring, responsible hands with their coaches. A former player who claimed she had a three-year relationship with Piazza that was limited to kissing and hugging said, "We did not dare tell our parents or anyone else, as we knew our parents would never allow us to play for Southington High and the coaches again." Another former player said, "My parents would have killed me if I went to them. And I don't think anyone at school would have believed me."

6. As in other cases of sexual misconduct, victims who do come forward often are not believed and are subjected to hostile reactions in both the school and the community. They are often perceived as troublemakers out to undermine community icons and the reputation of the school. The result is that the victims suffer so that other victims are afraid to come forward.

THE CASE OF DAN MARINO

In early November 1999, forty-four-year-old Dan Marino was a star teacher. He was the coach of the boys' football team, assistant coach of the girls' lacrosse team, and gym teacher at New Hyde Park High School, one of the high schools in the Sewanhaka Central High School District in Nassau County, New York. His football team had just won the Nassau County championship. He was an icon in the community, someone the students, parents, and community members looked up to, a professional who was guiding New Hyde Park athletic teams into county and state prominence.

His iconic status changed on November 10, when Marino was suddenly transferred to teach gym at another school in the district because of allegations that he had an improper relationship with a female student.[10] Jean Fichtl, a school board member, said, "Dan Marino was transferred to break the connection to a student with whom district officials believe he had a voluntary, one-on-one relationship. The transfer is the strongest action that the district could take because the school had limited evidence."

Marino's first reaction to the transfer was not unlike those of other teachers whose sexual misconduct becomes known. His response, according to Kreytak and Sarra, was "Rumors are rumors. They can really hurt a good man and his family." Marino was married with two children. However, school officials challenged the credibility of his response by indicating they believed a seventeen-year-old senior girl had a close relationship with Marino in which the two spent extended periods of time together off campus.

Marino was fired as football coach two days before New Hyde Park's regular season finale, a game the team won to finish with a record of 7–1. His record in fourteen seasons at New Hyde Park was 87–27 and he led the school to the conference title game three times in the 1990s.

The Sewanhaka High School District's response to alleged sexual misconduct was not unlike that of other school districts to such behavior. They transferred him to another school. As school board member Fichtl said, "To remove a teacher under tenure is very difficult." And remember, Marino was a community icon.

He had taken his football team to three conference title games in the 1990s and won the coveted title in 1999. When he stated, "Rumors are rumors. They can hurt a good man and his family," perhaps he was sending a message that he held a position of power in the community and he was not going quietly.

The investigation proceeded and, according to Kreytak and Sarra, while the district's union leaders were ostensibly backing Marino and saying his employment was not in jeopardy, the union contract allowed the school board to vote to begin proceedings to fire a teacher under several circumstances, including "engaging in conduct unbecoming a teacher" and "moral turpitude."

In the end the allegations of sexual misconduct against Marino were found to be true. In early March 2000, he was arrested and charged with statutory rape of the girl, a felony punishable by up to four years in prison. The police charged that Marino and the seventeen-year-old had consensual sex in September 1999 at the Sunrise Motel in nearby Lynbrook.[11]

Although he was arrested for that one incident, according to police it was believed that the sexual encounters happened more than once as they often met off campus and during the summer months. Yet Marino served no jail time. Marino admitted he carried on a sexual relationship with the girl from February 1999 until his arrest in March 2000, four months after school officials suspected something was wrong.[12]

Marino's lawyer, Brian Davis, said, "This was an aberrant occurrence. He's not a predator. This has never happened before." Marino was placed on probation for three years and forced to resign his teaching position and surrender his New York State teaching license. There are many lessons to be learned from the Dan Marino case.

Clearly Marino was at risk of becoming involved in crossing boundaries and sexual misconduct. The conditions for such activity were present. For one, the relationship began in February 1999, when Marino became assistant coach of the girls' lacrosse team. Here was a man whose entire coaching experience had been with male students. Did he have any training to prepare him to work with female students in the close relationships required in coaching?

And what about his personal needs? Yes, he was married and had two children. But did he have unmet personal needs? I know from my own experience as a high school educator and sports fan that football coaches spend a great deal of time away from their families, holding practices, scouting and watching films of coming opponents, meeting with college recruiters, and often seeking relief from the pressure to win games by hanging out with fellow coaches to socialize.

It's a clubby atmosphere that often does not include partners and serves as a home away from home for overextended coaches. Coaching then can spawn a negative home relationship in which partners, wives, and children are increasingly left on their own, abandoned, and marriages become at risk.

We don't know about Dan Marino's home life, but when he became involved as a girls' high school coach he ignored professional boundaries and the warning light of danger ahead. He met with the girl for extended periods of time off campus during the summer months and eventually risked having sex with her in a local motel. He appears to have been blinded by the relationship and was perhaps naïvely confident that his power role as football coach left him free to pursue such risky behavior. Yet someone had to notice.

Weren't there fellow coaches, girls on the lacrosse team, colleagues, administrators, or parents to observe a successful professional and a love-struck teenager headed for trouble? Clearly there was enough evidence, although the school board's initial reaction was to say there was "limited evidence," even though they had reason to be suspicious.

Here was a highly successful teacher who went down a wrong road and ended up ruining his career and harming a vulnerable student, his wife, and his two children. Training, supervision, monitoring, and intervention might have saved Dan Marino from this tragic end.

However, there are educators like Dan Marino who are icons and stars in their school district and believe that boundaries, rules, and regulations don't apply to them. One of the major lessons from the Dan Marino case is that coaches may be the most vulnerable group to sexual misconduct as they feel "untouchable" and beyond reach of any retribution.

THE CASE OF JOHN SHOCKRO

John Shockro was a popular teacher and coach for twenty-seven years at Old Rochester Regional Junior and Senior High Schools in Mattapoisett, Massachusetts. However, Shockro had a dark side to his personality. He sexually assaulted a number of young women during his career. In 2003, he pleaded guilty to seven counts of child rape and six other sexual assault charges involving two students from 1994 through 1996. At least eight more students and ex-students were waiting to testify to their similar abuse but the hearings never went that far.[13]

How did a popular teacher, coach, and coordinator of the town's recreation program pursue his sexual misconduct without intervention by the school committee, administration, colleagues, or community leaders? The Old Rochester school community is relatively small: 2,700 students from the towns of Marion, Mattapoisett, and Rochester, with a population of 15,000 residents. These are tight-knit communities where people are known to each other.

The school administrators and school committee turned a deaf ear to the wails of the injured children, and the system put in place to protect children betrayed them, valuing sportsmanship, political ties, and the usual tendency to victimize the victims in such cases over truth and the grim reality that John Shockro was an at-risk educator out to sexually abuse vulnerable students.

Why did otherwise responsible adults enable Shockro to prey on young women unhindered and stand by him throughout the trial intoning his good character, community service, and total inability to commit such abominable acts? Where were the training, supervision, monitoring, and intervention that might have stopped John Shockro from his damaging and dangerous behaviors early in his career? Where was the intervention for many vulnerable young women? Why were they unable to raise their voices and be heard?

I believe that one of John Shockro's victims provides answers to these questions.[14] Teachers like Shockro who prey on vulnerable students often seek out students who are undergoing great stress, need adult attention, can be intimidated by threats, are less likely to be believed, and in the end are easy marks and low risks.

During Shockro's trial the teenage girl talked about trust, betrayal, and the pain of a community that refused to believe her report, a school that turned its back on her. The teenager who told school officials in 1995 that the junior high gym teacher raped her said she was shunned by friends and community members who all rallied behind that longtime basketball coach when the allegations were made.

She said nearly everyone in town was convinced she was lying and that the brain tumor she suffered made her delusional. "Two out of 6,000 people believed me," she said. "My self-respect turned into self-loathing. Nobody would believe Coach Shockro would do this. Abuse isn't supposed to happen in a town like ours." Only after a second victim came forward, followed by eight more, did some people begin to believe what she told school officials the year before.

The second victim, who was just thirteen when first sexually assaulted by Shockro, said she was a vulnerable girl befriended by a man admired in both the community and the school. His attention was flattering, but when the attention turned to sex, it was frightening, she said. Both girls said they were the ones who shouldered the blame when the allegations were finally made public. They said other students called them whores and liars.

One girl attempted suicide and wound up in a trauma hospital. Fortunately some adults did believe these young women and were able to intervene and offer a lifeline of support. One of those adults was Detective Mary Lyons of the Mattapoisett Police Department.

On February 7, 1997, Lyons sat behind a one-way mirror at the South Bay Mental Health Center in Plymouth, Massachusetts, and listened to Shockro's sixteen-year-old victim detail three years of rape and sexual assaults.[15] From that day she began a fact-finding odyssey that uncovered a town secret whispered about for years. Soon after hearing from the first victim, she learned the name of another teenager raped by Shockro.

As word spread about the investigation, calls began coming in to the police station. There were more victims. Some left names. Some left phone numbers. Some left other information. Lyons became an investigative team of one in a case that divided the town between believers in the children and believers in the coach, who wore white ribbons to show their support.

In the end eight young women agreed to testify in the case to back up the two teenagers' allegations, strikingly familiar stories of being seduced by Shockro. Gentle words and friendship were followed by kisses and then rape in the locker room, his office, and his beach house. The rape often involved punching the girls if they resisted. Where was the school official charged with ensuring these young women's safety? Who knew what—and when?[16] One of the victims, aged sixteen at the time of the attack in the boys' locker room, told high school athletic director Joao Rodriguez about it the following day.

According to the police, Rodriguez accompanied the girl to a female guidance counselor and at some point an assistant principal was made aware of the allegations. Old Rochester Regional High School Principal James Eagan said in February 1997 that his staff took appropriate measures at the time and those school officials who heard the girl's report firsthand in 1995 did not believe it fit the description of a crime. But there is more to this story.

School officials seemingly chose to protect Shockro rather than the young woman. Maureen Boyle reports that Detective Mary Lyons indicated that the teenage victim and her parents had pressed complaints about Shockro to school officials, but had been told to stop talking about the rape and Mr. Shockro or face disciplinary action or suspension. And while school officials knew about the incident, it was not reported to the Massachusetts Department of Social Service or police, as required by law. Meanwhile, Shockro was reprimanded with a written warning from Superintendent Walsh.[17]

As Detective Lyons observed, "People had to know. Maybe they didn't say anything because there was no proof. Maybe they didn't want to believe it." A lot of people knew. Some of the girls who were teenagers twenty years ago were still in town. The people who "knew" included athletic director Joao Rodriguez, junior high principal Robert Gardner, guidance counselor Barbara Meehan, assistant high school principal Carol Stigh, high school principal Eagan, assistant superintendent Carol Young, and superintendent Walsh. Where were the training, supervision, monitoring, and intervention that might have raised a red flag and put a stop to Shockro's ongoing sexual misconduct?

Instead Shockro was treated as a deity and left to act out. As Detective Lyons said, Shockro's standing in the community provided a cloak of immunity and respectability. "He was with the in crowd," she said. "He was an icon in the community." He was a good father, family man, and churchgoer, involved in youth activities. He was a star in the school and the community and often stars begin to believe in their special status and ignore boundaries.

And where was the intervention for Shockro's victim? The young woman and her parents came forward with a story of a rape in the locker room and she was threatened with suspension. Powerful forces were at play to silence the young woman and those victims that followed. No one with the power to stop Shockro appeared to care about the poor victims and the ongoing hell they were going through. And, as I have suggested, one question left unanswered is what kind of power Shockro had over those educators who looked the other way to his reckless abusing of vulnerable students.

This case demonstrates how we all, including Old Rochester educators Gardner, Rodriguez, Meehan, Stigh, Eagan, Young, and Walsh, can be blinded by our allegiance and trust in our star teachers even when the red light of danger is flashing for all to see. Could Shockro have been asking to be found out as he took more and more risks by having sex in his office, the locker room, and his beach house and was unable to stop himself? He probably knew that some colleagues, administrators, students, and community members were aware of his destructive behaviors.

Ignoring or allowing John Shockro to continue his sexual misconduct came at great cost to his victims and their families, the reputation of the Old Rochester school district, the district's top management team, the professional staff, community advocates and watchdog groups, and junior high principal Robert Gardner, who retired in 1997.

Gardner should have a plaque and letters bearing his name adorn the auditorium at Old Rochester Regional High School, where he was principal for three decades.[18] Instead Gardner asked school officials to scrape his name from the wall after fresh allegations were released that he had ignored complaints about gym teacher John Shockro, who pleaded guilty in 1997 to raping two students. Over Christmas 2004, officials planned to quietly remove Gardner's name at his request.

But the question of whether he should be honored still divides residents of Marion, Mattapoisett, and Rochester. Some believe Gardner should be honored for his long career. Others say any memorial to his service would become an indelible reminder of one of the region's most wrenching episodes. "Gardner has a legacy and it shouldn't be on the auditorium, because it will just remind people of the injustice done to girls over time," said Dede Smith. "The school didn't do its job when Gardner was at the helm."

In addition to not doing his job, Gardner viewed female students as suspect and given to fantasizing about sexual relationships with staff. He also swept aside Shockro's own statements that he kissed, hugged, and swore at his victims. According to reporter Michael Levinson, Gardner testified at Shockro's trial that he did not know that one of Shockro's victims, Kristen Canty, had alleged she was raped in 1996.

He said he only knew that Shockro had kissed her, hugged her, and swore at her. Gardner told the court that he believed many high school girls were "a different breed of cat" and he believed Canty was fantasizing. Even after another student came forward in 1997 with concrete evidence that Shockro had sexually assaulted her, Gardner did not revisit Canty's allegations. He testified instead, accepting Shockro's assurances, that "nothing untoward" had occurred.

Gardner's response to a petition by community residents to remove the plaque was "I have been the designated sin-eater for the past ten years and I am really tired of it. It's just too much." The Old Rochester School and the community remain divided over who knew what and when. Questions still abound. Community resident Cathrene Foren of Marion suggests that if Gardner "had a glimmer of what was going on, that would be tragic."

The one constant in the revelations about Shockro has been the testimony of former students at the school. Hearing their assessment leaves little doubt that, as Cathrene Foren and Dede Smith suggest, "The school didn't do its job when Gardner was at the helm." A former student of Shockro described his behaviors, saying, "He set up an office in the boys' locker room, girls used to visit there at lunchtime and all kinds of crazy stuff happened. They shouldn't have been in there." It's too bad the leaders of the Old Rochester schools didn't have that wisdom. "They shouldn't have been in there," says it all.

THE WASHINGTON STATE STORY OF COACHES' SEXUAL MISCONDUCT

This final section on coaches' sexual misconduct borrows on the yearlong research of *Seattle Times* reporters Christine Willmsen and Maureen O'Hagan that culminated in a series titled "Coaches Who Prey," which ran in December 2003 and January 2004.[19] In review, their study supports many of the aspects of my sexual misconduct profile for coaches at risk. The data also documents how some educators involved in unchecked sexual misconduct move on to adopt a predatory lifestyle and prey on vulnerable students while believing they will not be challenged, confronted, or fired, such as the cases and issues I discuss in chapter 4 on teachers as predators.

Willmsen and O'Hagan's research offers a clear picture of the problem and the kinds of variables, like the advent of Title IX, that helped to create such misconduct. Here is what they found. They report that over the past decade, 159 coaches in Washington have been fired or reprimanded for sexual misconduct ranging from harassment to rape. Nearly all were male coaches involved with female students. At least ninety-five of these coaches continue to teach or coach.

The number of offending coaches is actually much greater because, when faced with complaints against coaches, school officials often failed to investigate them and sometimes ignored a law requiring them to report suspected abuse to police.

Even after being caught, many men were allowed to continue coaching because school administrators promised to keep their disciplinary records secret if the coaches simply left. Some districts paid tens of thousands of dollars to get coaches to leave. Other districts hired coaches they knew had records of sexual misconduct. The research also focused on the growing field of club teams, such as the Colorado Hoopsters described in the Rick Lopez case.

They found that coaches could get a job or start a team with almost no regulation or oversight. They also found that many parents ignored the warning signs of sexual misconduct. As in the Rick Lopez case, some parents suspected misconduct and did little to stop it, trusting the coaches while doubting their accusers.

As Willmsen and O'Hagan report, "Unfortunately, everyone has an investment in the silence, the parents, the team and community," said Sandra Kirby, a Canadian sociologist who studied sexual abuse of athletes by coaches. "The measure is, if a coach has good success, that's all they worried about. They're ignoring the victim." The research also points out the demand for quality coaching in girls' sports that burgeoned when Congress passed Title IX, requiring that girls be given the same educational and athletic opportunities as boys.

The number of girls playing high school sports in Washington tripled since 1972. In 2002, 43 percent of high school girls played sports. That doesn't include the thousands of girls who take part in recreational and club teams outside the school setting. The boom created a nearly insatiable call for coaches, most of whom were men, coaches whom Willmsen and O'Hagan describe as being in a demanding profession with long hours, often low pay, and pressure from insistent fans.

And for most of the more than twenty thousand coaches in Washington State, the reward is the satisfaction of mentoring student athletes, not only in the skills of a particular sport, but also in the values of teamwork, practice, and sportsmanship. However, Willmsen and O'Hagan suggest that there is a potential downside to such close contact that can span many years. They point out that coaching presents a unique opportunity for sexual misconduct.

Coaches work with athletes for hours at a time, often over several years, in unstructured situations such as locker rooms or out-of-town tournaments. Kids and parents generally admire them. But the research of Willmsen and O'Hagan shows that Washington teachers who coach are three times more likely to be investigated by the state for sexual misconduct.

As in the cases of Joe Sutton, Rick Lopez, Dan Marino, and John Shockro, many of the coaches were, as O'Hagan and Willmsen suggest, "big celebrities,"[20] who at first became involved in sexual misconduct and then moved on to adopt predatory lifestyles as coaches because they were allowed great leeway, for example, by moving from school district to school district and from one victim to another.

Let's examine the case of Randy Deming, a successful wrestling coach in Blaine, Washington, who won state coach of the year honors in 1990. When district officials suspended the coach in 1990 for allegedly rubbing a student's breasts and touching her genital area, people circulated petitions asking the school not to terminate him.

The school district charges against him were dropped when he accepted an offer to resign in March 1991. Still, he went on to coach at Mount Adams White Swan High School, which wanted a top wrestling coach and hired

Deming in 1995 despite his background, according to O'Hagan and Willmsen. However, Deming didn't change his troublesome conduct.

Girls there complained of unwanted touching. Mount Adams officials disciplined him five times in the 2002–2003 school year. In March 2003, he was charged with two counts of fourth-degree assault with sexual motivation after allegedly touching two eighth-grade girls in his math class. After a three-day trial, jurors decided the coach's conduct was not criminal and acquitted him. Meanwhile, the Mount Adams School District gave Deming notice that he was going to be fired. He is appealing that decision and is on paid leave.

Then there is the case of Port Townsend basketball coach Randy Sheriff. As O'Hagan and Willmsen recount, the bond between a fifteen-year-old Port Townsend girl and the thirty-four-year-old Sheriff was especially strong. The girl, raised in a troubled home, saw Randy Sheriff not only as a mentor, but also as a surrogate parent and "the greatest dad in the world." Sheriff showered her with attention, then with flowers and chocolates, then with kisses. Before long the coach, a married man with two children, was sending the teenager love notes.

By the time she was sixteen, she says, they were having sex in his car, at his house, and in motels. She babysat his two children, was Sheriff's coaching assistant for the boys' basketball team, and accompanied him on road trips. She trained with him at his California basketball camp and he took her to Australia with an adult men's team. The girl reported, "I felt puzzled, like I was falling in love. He was my lifeline." According to Heather Carter, a Port Townsend graduate, "Everyone in school knew they were having an affair."

Although the Port Townsend school officials believed Sheriff was having an intimate relationship with her, according to Willmsen and O'Hagan, they simply nudged him out of town, allowing him to land a coaching job in the Cascade Mountain town of Cle Elum, where he was accused of preying on another girl.

The girl sued the Port Townsend district and they settled with her for $50,000 in 2002. Sheriff settled for an undisclosed sum and was told he was no longer needed as the boys' basketball coach despite taking the team to the state tournament. Why was Randy Sheriff allowed to cross boundaries? As Heather Carter suggests, "everyone knew."

One reason is that Sheriff came to Port Townsend in 1983 with an impressive résumé. He had led Seattle's Roosevelt High School basketball team to the 1973 state tournament and played professional basketball in Europe. He was a star player and coach and, as we have seen in this chapter, star coaches are often given great leeway. According to Willmsen and O'Hagan, Randy Sheriff still denies the charges.

According to O'Hagan and Willmsen, Detective Joe Beard, who is in charge of sex offender notification in the Snohomish County Sheriff's Office, said that school administrators, as well as parents, need better training in identifying and acting on signs of sexual abuse.[21] Beard is right. Tim Flannery, assistant director of the National Federation of State High School Associations (NFHS), puts it well when he suggests, "The only way we can slow sexual misconduct down is to educate coaches on their role and responsibility. Training becomes critical. School and state associations should make it mandatory for coaches to get this training."[22]

As publications of the Women's Sports Foundation point out, romantic and/or sexual relationships between coaches and athletes compromise the professional integrity of the coach and the educational mission of athletics. The foundation suggests that coaches need to be provided with information, training, and continuing education about how power, dependence, "love," and sexual attraction can influence coach–athlete relationships. Upper-level administrators need to take responsibility for organizing educational and training sessions for coaches and staff.

However, the Washington Interscholastic Activities Association (WIAA), which oversees athletics in the state's nearly three hundred school districts, has not addressed sexual misconduct in the clinics its member coaches are required to attend. "The association tells coaches how to tape ankles, prevent injuries, motivate athletes, even deal with the media, but not how to keep proper boundaries with young players." There is work to be done to ensure that coaches and teachers receive the kind of training they and their students deserve.

Chapter 4 will present cases of sexual misconduct that involve predator teachers, professionals who clearly set out to lure vulnerable students into unwanted sexual acts to satisfy their own emotional and sexual needs. As these case studies demonstrate, predator teachers are not difficult to identify. Think about the cases of Randy Deming and Randy Sheriff that Willmsen and O'Hagan so vividly describe. "Everybody knew," including administrators, teachers, students, and parents.

Predators lure students into relationships often using the guise of mentoring and coaching. But these kinds of predatory acts are different from those that may be a by-product of an intense coach–athlete relationship. Predatory relationships are not rooted in friendship and love. There is no bonding, caring, or deep relationship in these cases. They involve only using, abusing, threatening, and damaging the victims.

NOTES

1. Robin Finn, "Growth in Women's Sports Stirs Harassment Issues," *New York Times*, March 7, 1999, 1 (A), 24 (L).
2. Finn, "Growth in Women's Sports Stirs Harassment Issues."
3. Adam Thompson, "Summer Tourneys Where It's at for College Hopefuls," *Denver Post*, October 12, 2003, http://www.denverpost.com/Stories/0.1413.36%7E76

%1680740.00.html.

4. Adam Thompson and Bill Briggs, "Sex Charges Shadow Girls' Coach," *Denver Post*, October 12, 2003, http://www.denverpost.com/cda/article/print/0.1674.36%7E76%7E1693470.00.html.

5. DenverChannel.com, "Girls' Basketball Coach May Face 100 Counts Related to Sexual Assaults," August 20, 2004, http://www.thedenverchannel.com/print/3669544/detail.html.

6. Mary Ellen Fillo, "Shadows Stalked Girls' Glory Days," Associated Press, March 10, 2002, 5–7 (A1).

7. Kimberly W. Moy and William Schubert, "Coaches Avoid Charges in Sex Allegations," *Hartford Courant*, January 10, 2002, 7 (A1).

8. *Hartford Courant* editorial, "End Mr. McKernan's Career," *Hartford Courant*, June 4, 2004, 10 (A).

9. *Southington Journal*, "Town's Disgust Outlasts a Statute of Limitations," *New York Times*, January 14, 2002, 17 (A).

10. Steven Kreytak and Gregg Sarra, "'Connection' Broken," *Newsday*, November 11, 1999, 5, 60 (A).

11. Steven Kreytak, "Gym Teacher Charged with Rape," *Newsday*, March 8, 2000, 8 (A).

12. Chau Lam, "No Jail for Coach in Affair," *Newsday*, March 21, 2000, 29 (A).

13. Mary Ann Sorrentino, "John Shockro Not the Only Guilty Party in Sordid Case," *South Coast Today*, January 7, 1998, http://www.s-t.com/daily/01-07-98/c04op105.htm.

14. Maureen Boyle and Bridgette Sweeney, "From Trust to Betrayal and Lingering Pain," *South Coast Today*, December 31, 1997, http://southcoasttoday.com/daily/12-97/12-31-97/a01lo0005.htm.

15. Maureen Boyle, "Detective Lyons Investigated Shockro Case 'Relentlessly,'" *South Coast Today*, January 8, 1998, http://www.s-t.com/daily/01-98/01-08/a01o003.htm.

16. Ellen O'Brien, "Police Press Questions to School in Rape Case," *Boston Sunday Globe*, February 16, 1997, 4 (B).

17. John Estrella, "10 Days of Allegations, Questions, and Headlines," *South-Coast Today*, February 23, 1997, http://www.southcoasttoday.com/daily/02-97/02-23-97/a011o005.htm.

18. Michael Levinson, "Ex-Principal Rejects Naming Honor," *Boston*, December 12, 2004, http://boston.com/news/local/articles/2004/ex_principal_rejects_naming_hon.

19. Christine Willmsen and Maureen O'Hagan, "Coaches Continue Working for Schools and Private Teams after Being Caught for Sexual Misconduct," *Seattle Times*, December 14, 2000, http://seattletimes.nwsource.com/news/local/coaches/news/dayone.html.

20. Maureen O'Hagan and Christine Willmsen, "Misconduct Often Goes Unpunished by Districts," *Seattle Times*, December 15, 2003, http://seattletimes.nwsource.com/news/local/coaches/news/daytwo.html.

21. Maureen O'Hagan and Christine Willmsen, "What School Districts Can Do," *Seattle Times*, December 15, 2003, http://seattletimes.nwsource.com/news/local/coaches/news/schools.html.

22. Christine Willmsen and Maureen O'Hagan, "Misconduct Registry, More Training Needed for Washington Coaches," *Seattle Times*, December 16, 2003, http://seattletimes/nwsource.com/news/local/coaches/news/state.html.

Chapter Four

Cases of Predator Teachers

William Swiggart suggests in his study of sexual misconduct among physicians that there are four categories of offenders. The lovesick physician, who may feel normal ethical guidelines do not apply in matters of love. These physicians appear healthy but may be experiencing significant life crises; the limitless physician, with tireless and selfish devotion to patients, who may be vulnerable to the demands of difficult patients. This physician avoids conflict and has almost no ability to limit patients' requests. The predatory physician, who represents small but notorious groups of physicians' misconduct cases that are associated with severe narcissistic and antisocial personality disorders. The psychotic physician, who represents the smallest group, is the truly mentally ill physician.[1]

Swiggart's categories are helpful in our study of teacher sexual misconduct. The focus of this chapter is on a small but notorious group of educators who appear to be predators and in some cases mentally ill. What is startling in these cases, as in the cases in chapters 2 and 3, is the lack of response by administrators and colleagues, even when students clearly observed that behavior was well out of the norm.

These case studies once again demonstrate the need for administrators and teachers to look closely at the behavior of teachers who are at risk of abusing their students and not turn a blind eye. A review of these cases offers a beginning profile of educators who are predators or on the road to such damaging behavior. Here is an assessment of a beginning profile.

Predator teachers are not interested in close emotional relationships with students. Their goal is to satisfy their own sexual needs. They may pretend to offer friendship, a role as a surrogate parent, an adult role model, or even a lover, but their main goal is carrying out a sexual relationship with naïve and vulnerable students.

Because they have done it many times, predator teachers are highly skilled at luring needy students into their web of abuse.

Predator teachers often don't benefit from training, supervision, and intervention because their main goal is involving an ongoing number of students in sexual relationships. However, training, supervision, and intervention are highly useful to administrators and staff members in identifying and rooting out predator teachers.

Predator teachers often seek out students who are undergoing great stress, need adult attention, can be intimidated, and are less likely to be believed if they cry out for help. These students are easy targets and at low risk to seek help.

Predator teachers use the threat of blaming the victim, brand the victim as the aggressor and a liar, and use physical force and intimidation to keep their victims in an abusive relationship.

Predator teachers can be powerful star teachers or coaches who are renowned in their school districts and are major contributors to the district's success and reputation. Their predatory behaviors, while known in the school and community, are allowed to go unchecked because of their powerful positions. Their student victims are thus reluctant to come forward, and those who do are often not believed or are pressured to be silent.

Many predator teachers are allowed to transfer from school to school even though their predatory behaviors are known by the sender schools. Often they continue their sexual abuse of students in each new school. It is an ongoing pattern of sexual misconduct.

Predator teachers use their teaching, advising, and coaching relationships with needy students to lure them into sexual relationships.

Predator teachers are not afraid of carrying out extremely risky behavior in that they often become involved in sexual relationships with students in the school building, motels, the victim's home, and in their own homes.

When reprimanded for their behavior, predator teachers use sophisticated tactics to plead their innocence such as blaming the victim.

In some school settings, there is a climate that turns a blind eye to predatory sexual misconduct by teachers and coaches in spite of ongoing rumors of such behaviors in the school community. Here are the cases.

THE CASE OF MICHAEL DWAYNE BLEVINS

Michael Dwayne Blevins was a teacher and coach in Wytheville, Virginia. In 1998, he was charged with sexually abusing three young women. One girl from Rural Retreat High was involved with him for more than four years, even after he left Wythe County for Shawnsville Middle and High School in

Montgomery County, Virginia.[2] He became involved with two other seventeen year olds at Shawnsville.

In each case he played on the girl's sympathy and then won greater access by asking her to spend extra time with him to enter statistics into a computer. At Rural Retreat, the computer was in his private office in the high school wrestling room, while at Shawnsville it was in his apartment.

"It was always, 'Poor me. I need all the mothering and comforting,'" said Sandra Wright, an assistant prosecutor in Montgomery County, one of the three counties where Blevins pleaded guilty to sex charges. "And they fell for it." For example, the student from Rural Retreat High School said about Blevins, "He told me I was the one person he could always trust. He'd just single me out and make me feel good." She in turn assured him by saying, "If you ever need somebody to talk to, you can talk to me."

And Blevins did, manipulating the young woman into a deeper relationship by indicating he needed her to help resolve his suicidal thoughts. It was a relationship that eventually led to sex in his office in the high school wrestling room. Blevins was sentenced in December 1998 to serve twenty-five years in prison.

Some experts say one reason some adults are drawn to adolescents and younger children is that they are so easy to manipulate. For example, "If you try to approach an adult, it can be scary," said Robert Prentky, the director of assessment at the Justice Resource Center in Massachusetts. "It's far less likely that a child is going to reject you."

W. Richard Fossey, dean of the college of education at Louisiana State University, suggests that predators like Blevins "have an uncanny ability to pick a child who is needy, has poor communication with his or her parents and is a kid who isn't going to tell." Students who lack strong relations with parents and peers or face unusual stress may be more receptive to the attention and more intimidated by threats.

Edward Stancik, the special commissioner for the New York City school system, asserts, "It's also because they're less likely to be believed. They're seen as an easy mark and low risk." Michael Dwayne Blevins fits our profile of the predator teacher. His major goal is to satisfy his sexual desires, not form a helping relationship. Richard Fossey suggests that he had the uncanny ability to pick a child who was needy, had poor communication with her parents, and was a kid who wasn't going to tell. A kid who, as Edward Stancik suggests, was an easy mark and, most important, less likely to be believed if she came forward and asked for help.

Our secondary schools are filled with students like this. Some are needy teens at the margins of school life that have a pattern of continuous failure and acting out behavior. They are often anonymous and written off as on their way to dropping out. Others are successful students who have troubled home lives and estranged relationships with parents that they keep to themselves, not students you would expect to have troubles and most certainly not be involved in a sexual relationship with a teacher.

Both groups are vulnerable to drifting into risky relationships because their need for caring adult contact is so great, relationships that again are often obvious to observing students whose suspicion is aroused by the close contact between the teacher and student but not recognized by the victims involved. They see no warning signs or red light because they want so much to be loved and cared for.

THE CASE OF RICHARD PLASS

Richard Plass, a renowned teacher and assistant principal at Stuyvesant High School in New York City, was arrested on May 21, 1999, and charged with molesting a fifteen-year-old ninth-grade student who had volunteered to work as his assistant. Plass, fifty-five, had worked at Stuyvesant for the past sixteen years and taught in the city system for thirty-three years. The abuse took place in 1998 in Plass's office at the school.[3] During the first encounter, he attempted to rub the girl's leg and tried to hug her while he viewed pornographic websites.

The girl told investigators that she consistently rebuffed Plass's advances. On other occasions, Plass masturbated in the girl's presence and tried to touch her genitals. Investigators learned of the incidents from a teacher who read a journal that the girl was keeping as part of a class. In her entries, which were made in February 1999, the girl wrote about the incidents as if they were happening to a friend.

Plass was no ordinary teacher and Stuyvesant is no ordinary school. Plass, a biology teacher, was best known for encouraging students to enter the annual Westinghouse science competition, recently renamed Intel Science Talent Research. For sixteen years, he pushed students to enter the contest and then shepherded their progress through the entry procedure.

In his career at Stuyvesant, Plass oversaw 250 finalists and two dozen winners, more winners than any other high school in America. Stuyvesant, one of the elite high schools in New York City, has long been known for producing a number of finalists for the Intel program each year, helping fortify its reputation as one of the finest public schools in the country.

Plass was a star teacher in a star school. Bright and ambitious students flocked to Stuyvesant, hoping to gain enrollment in the highly coveted multi-year science program he administered in order to compete in the Intel competition. He and his program were a major drawing card for the best and brightest New York City students. He held the keys to which students entered and which students were rejected, and he could make or break students once they were in the program.

In a real sense he was his own boss and seemingly not subject to the rules and boundaries observed by colleagues. He was on his own, enthroned in a position of power in which he sexually abused and harassed students, knowing that if they spoke out he had the power to drop them from the program. The fifteen-year-old abused student had volunteered to help in Plass's office in hopes of entering the Intel program. However, she was only the latest of Plass's victims.

Investigators disclosed that other students in the Intel program reported that Plass had made inappropriate comments to them and looked down girls' shirts in class.[4] The students did not report the incidents because they feared the powerful teacher would kick them out.

Plass's predatory behavior was apparently known to school officials. In fact, Plass was allowed to transfer to Stuyvesant High from Grover Cleveland High School in Queens, New York, after complaints were filed against him for sexually harassing students there, complaints that could no longer be pursued because a three- to five-year statute of limitations in such cases had run out. At Stuyvesant complaints were filed against Plass by female students in 1985 and 1992, complaints that resulted only in a reprimand for Plass. In August 1999, Plass plead guilty to sexually harassing the fifteen-year-old student and received three years' probation as part of a plea bargain.

There are many obvious lessons in the Plass case. It serves as a reminder that despite its vaunted academic standing, Stuyvesant was as vulnerable as any other school to such acts.[5]

Students enrolled in highly competitive high schools and special programs often fear speaking out against teachers on whom they rely for entrance into coveted school programs, high grades, and recommendations for college. As student body president David Meadvin suggests, it is unfair to expect students to openly confront teachers like Plass, who hold so much power over them.

Administrators and colleagues can turn a blind eye to the predatory behaviors of powerful entrepreneur teachers like Plass, who are seen as deities and drawing cards to enhance the school's reputation and allowed to set their own personal agendas and boundaries. Although there were complaints against Plass in 1985 and 1992, all he received was a reprimand. Incredibly, he was applying to be the school's new principal and was interviewed for the job only days before his arrest in May 1999. He was in the club and apparently felt beyond reproach and detection, even qualified to become principal.

Students are aware of the behavior of predator teachers like Plass and want administrators and teachers to act. It simply can't be left up to the students alone to sound the alarm, particularly with a powerful teacher like Plass.

Predator teachers like Plass can avoid detection in large high schools that lack close teacher–student helping relationships. Stuyvesant is housed in a ten-story building and has an enrollment of 3,100 students. It is a school, as reported by Randall C. Archibold, in which students report that student–teacher relationships are never particularly warm and in which students have the reputation of doing anything they must in order to stay on the good side of faculty members. Students reported that Plass was not someone that they felt comfortable going to with their problems. Most students did not look at him as a friend or someone who could be supportive of their needs.

Many predators like Plass leave a trail. For example, like Michael Blevins, they have moved on from schools where they have been involved in sexual misconduct. Yet observing and caring teachers can intervene and help abused students even when a cry for help is disguised as an incident happening to a friend, as in the case of the fifteen-year-old student abused by Plass.

The Plass case, however, suggests another subtler, less obvious lesson. When sexual abuse involves a star teacher or coach, it has the potential to damage the reputation of the school, school district, and the star teachers involved. In these situations, the victim's cry for help may be less likely to be believed and the needs of the institution for survival take over in an "it can't happen here" response.

Stuyvesant senior David Meadvin, eighteen, zeroed in on this lesson when he said to reporter Andrew Jacob, "If the allegations are true they should be dealt with, but I hope this doesn't overshadow all the good things about the school." Meadvin is not talking about the damage to the lives of harassed students. He is talking about the institution and the potential damage to the school's reputation.

The need to help the students who are victims of these predators and to implement a training, supervision, monitoring, and intervention program to stop such behaviors collide with the self-serving aspects of school life. This self-serving approach argues, "How will this case hurt our reputation as a safe, student-centered learning environment with strong academic programs? How will this case impact on our enrollment and recruiting efforts? Will these incidents of harassment make our school appear less special and innovative?"

Yet as in the case of Richard Plass, there were caring and courageous adults, a teacher, who challenged the self-serving status quo and acted on behalf of the students involved. They refused to allow school leaders to ignore or blame the victim in order to prevent a crack in the school's reputation.

THE CASE OF JOHN SCHAENMAN

Some cases of alleged sexual misconduct by teachers blur the lines between innocent and some would say naïve teachers who go beyond the call of duty to act as mentors, advisers, and coaches for needy students and teachers who use their close relationships with students to lure them into unwanted sexual relationships. The case of John Schaenman raises some of the complicated issues that arise when teachers become involved in such close relationships with students.

We have no proof that Schaenman was a predator. In fact, he was found not guilty of charges that he took indecent liberties with a student. However, the case does point out the potential mischief that can occur when a highly regarded teacher sets his own questionable boundaries with students. Here is the story and the issues and implications involved when training, supervision, monitoring, and intervention are absent.

Schaenman was an elementary school teacher in New Hope, North Carolina.[6] He was also a soccer coach who spent time mentoring boys. He invited youngsters to play tennis with him, spend the night at his apartment, and take trips out of town. In 1993, a twenty-year-old man alleged that Schaenman took indecent liberties. While a judge dismissed the charges, the case made a lot of people, both parents and teachers, uncomfortable. Schaenman declined to comment, but many of his colleagues said he left himself open to attack by allowing students to spend the night at his apartment.

Kaufman reports that Elvia Walker, who has been an educator for twenty-nine years, said teachers could form close relationships with children without raising questions of impropriety. "I've had kids who could tell me anything," said Walker, principal of West Cary Middle School. "It never would have crossed my mind to have them spend the night. There was a line that I didn't cross and a line they didn't cross. If you are mature and old enough to teach, there are some givens."

Ann Majestic, the attorney for the Durham and Wake school systems, said she still doesn't recommend that schools dictate the level of appropriate contact because that could discourage any relationships whatsoever. "I advocate no dating, no romantic relationships, but all the community-based programs have the primary purpose of adult males spending time with students away from school." That's where schools face a conflict. They don't want to discourage teachers and volunteers from being role models for children.

Trinia Holeman, a colleague of Schaenman at New Hope Elementary, suggests, "It is important for children to see us as friends, human beings and role models. Sometimes in social situations they learn from us not so much about academics but life. As teachers we want to touch the lives of children." Teachers who go beyond what is expected of them in the classroom, such as taking students on trips or even into their homes to work on projects, are often considered the best.

Schaenman also fits the profile of teachers at risk for sexual misconduct. He blurred the boundaries between his professional and personal life by inviting students to spend the night at his apartment, spent much of his free time mentoring boys, and took them on trips out of town. As his colleagues suggested, he was inviting trouble and leaving himself open to attack. He appeared to ignore or was unable to see the red light of danger as he engaged in these activities. He didn't put in place a line, as Elvia Walker suggests, that "I didn't cross and they didn't cross . . . there are some givens."

Schaenman's risky behavior was either ignored by parents, colleagues, and administrators or, as in the case of some parents, praised because they reported that Schaenman was a wonderful influence on their children. But clearly Schaenman operated on his own until he was charged with indecent liberties. Schaenman was cleared and returned to teaching.

This case illuminates the problems that can occur when adult male or female teachers who lack training, supervision, monitoring, and the necessary intervention when sexual misconduct is a possibility become involved as mentors for students. Educators and parents in the Triangle area of Raleigh, North Carolina, say there is a need to establish boundaries between adults and students outside the classroom, but there is no consensus on where to draw the line. Elvia Walker's response that "if you're mature and old enough to teach, there are some givens," while sounding like welcome advice, isn't enough to help some teachers establish boundaries and avoid sexual misconduct.

We are not talking here about age and maturity. Being an adult and mature by community standards does little to prepare teachers for the complicated professional and personal issues that emerge when they are asked to serve as role models, mentors, advisers, personal advocates for students, and so on.

Whatever title we bestow on teachers, it is incumbent on us to prepare them for how to handle these roles and encourage them to reach out for help when they find themselves crossing boundaries. Unfortunately age and maturity are of little help when the personal needs of teachers meet the personal needs of students head-on, especially as in the case of Schaenman, where there is no one listening and help isn't on the way until it's too late.

THE CASE OF KENNETH DELUCA

According to the Ontario (Canada) Province Ministry of Attorney General's report on April 9, 1996, Kenneth DeLuca plead guilty to fourteen sexual offenses involving thirteen victims.[7] The crimes took place between 1972 and 1993. Each was committed while DeLuca was a teacher with Sault Ste. Marie Roman Catholic School Board. All of his victims were females; all but one was a student. Their ages ranged from ten to eighteen. The report suggests that DeLuca represents the ultimate breach of the trust placed in a teacher—a teacher who preys on students.

However, as we have seen in many of the cases presented in this book, DeLuca's predatory behavior was known early on by administrators, colleagues, and parents. As early as 1973, and at numerous times thereafter, complaints were made about DeLuca's conduct to principals, other teachers, and school board officials. Though the complaints were well founded, they were not acted on. DeLuca's sexual misconduct continued for twenty years as he easily moved from school to school.

The report confirms that DeLuca's case was not unique and follows a pattern similar to other sexual misconduct cases. For example, teachers were reluctant to report suspected sexual misconduct by a colleague, victims and their parents were intimidated to prevent or discourage disclosure, misconduct was not acted on, and the suspected predator was transferred from school to school.

As the report states, "The response of the School Board and its employees to complaints or disclosures made by the victims was completely inadequate and, indeed, harmful. It involved, at times, stereotypical notions of what could be expected from a truthful victim, a minimizing of the seriousness of DeLuca's misconduct, a lack of objectivity and a self-serving approach to these complaints."

The report cites a review of the DeLuca case begun in May 1999 by Sydney J. Robins, a former judge of the Court of Appeals for Ontario, which resulted in 101 recommendations for change that specifically address "teacher–student sexual misconduct in the elementary and secondary schools."[8] This review supports five major arguments I make in this book by stating the following:

> The vast majority of teachers are unquestionably highly dedicated and caring professionals who seek to ensure a safe learning environment.
>
> There is no typical offence or offender in sexual misconduct cases. While sexual misconduct by teachers is perpetrated overwhelmingly by males, and overwhelmingly against females, it occurs in all combinations of gender. The popular conception that anyone who sexually abuses a child is a pedophile is simply wrong. In fact, teachers who engage in sexual misconduct with children and adolescents are not pedophiles in most cases. For example, terms such as "boundary violators," "romantic-bad judgment abusers" or "situational offenders" have been used to describe different types of abusers.
>
> Students abused by teachers probably delay disclosure by reason of deference to an authority figure, embarrassment, guilt and fear—fear of retaliation by the abuser, fear that no one will believe them, fear of being blamed and fear of some sort of punishment. A child's desire to comply with the request of an adult he or she trusts and by whom he or she wishes to be accepted is another inhibitor of disclosure. The genuine affection a child may have for the teacher, especially one who promotes the "special relationship" and who has spent a great deal of time in the grooming phase, should not be underestimated.

Teachers fear that a heightened sensitivity to potential accusations of sexual misconduct will have a chilling effect on a friendly and nurturing school environment. They are no doubt appalled by conduct such as Kenneth DeLuca's and are understandably concerned that such conduct may unfairly reflect upon them and their profession.

It must be concluded that the DeLuca case is neither aberrant nor out of date. Teacher sexual misconduct is sufficiently prevalent to warrant special attention. Arguments to the contrary should not be allowed to forestall efforts to understand the problem and actively address it.

Sexual misconduct doesn't just happen. As the case studies in chapters 2 through 4 suggest, sexual misconduct occurs in an environment in which teachers and coaches are allowed to operate on their own without needed training, supervision, monitoring, and intervention. They are allowed to cross boundaries even when their destructive behavior is observed by administrators, colleagues, students, parents, and community members.

These otherwise responsible members of the school community are seemingly frozen into inaction by the behaviors involved in sexual misconduct, as are the victims. It's an "it can't happen here" mentality. They look the other way, don't speak out, and tend to mistrust their own sound judgment, particularly when the misconduct involves a star teacher or coach and students, who as Old Rochester Junior High principal Robert Gardner describes, are erroneously labeled as given to sexual fantasies.

This is a process that blames the victim who comes forward and defends the abusing educator until he or she is pursued and the truth becomes known. Yes, some of these case studies reveal that there are examples of some educators being falsely accused. But school administrators need to be careful, as in the Shockro case, not to be blindsided by long-held allegiances and, as in the case of Robert Gardner, their own biases.[9]

When sexual misconduct occurs, one of the most damaging aftermaths is the loss of faith and trust in adults in the school by students, parents, and even colleagues. Suspicion takes over. Teachers close their doors. Help for a needy student is harder to find. Rumors abound. In almost every situation—from the cases of Glenn Harris, Gwendolyn Hampton, and Dr. D (Alois Dlhopolsky) to the cases of Richard Plass, John Shockro, and Joseph Daddio and the Southington High School coaches—the school climate in which the misconduct occurred changed dramatically. Students and parents became more wary of teachers who were committed to helping their students resolve personal as well as academic problems.

As Southington resident Matthew Welinsky said, "You think you can trust teachers and that the children are safe and then you hear about something like this, going on without anyone noticing."[10] Many teachers, as a result of such observations, end up increasing their professional distance from needy students, avoid helping students with personal problems, and warn colleagues to focus on their academic teaching and leave the helping to the professional counselors.

In cases like Southington, often community-based counselors are brought in from outside agencies to temporarily offer support to students. Administrators become more vigilant. As current Southington superintendent Harvey Polansky said, "We will continue to ensure a safe environment for our students."[11] In the aftermath trust erodes between students and teachers, parents and teachers, teachers and teachers, and teachers and administrators.

However, often within a short time the community counselors leave and teachers close their doors to helping needy students. The result is a double whammy; the training, supervision, monitoring, and intervention that might have lowered the possibility of the sexual misconduct is still absent while the school climate becomes marked by suspicion and self-protection. The victims in this scenario are once again the needy, vulnerable students who desperately need a caring adult mentor and teachers who want to help these students.

As we proceed to chapter 5, with its emphasis on training, supervision, helpful peer observations, and intervention to solve the problem of sexual misconduct in the schools, let's summarize what we know about the problem, data that can help us formulate how best to proceed.

There is no "epidemic" of teacher sexual misconduct, but it is a problem that must be addressed.

Pedophiles and psychotics represent only a small percentage of teachers involved in sexual misconduct. They should be weeded out by effective early screening in the hiring and supervision process. The vast majority of teachers and coaches involved in sexual misconduct are otherwise successful professionals who find themselves ill-prepared to handle close contact with needy students. The major emphasis on solving the problem of sexual misconduct should be aimed at this latter group.

Training for teachers and coaches should focus on the notion that every teacher can be at risk of sexual misconduct given a clustering together of certain professional and personal circumstances. These may be family problems involving divorce, death, illness, and so on. Some teachers may unwittingly seek emotional connections through close personal involvement with equally needy students. A professional setback may also trigger the need for close involvement that is being denied in the adult world.

Teachers who serve as coaches, advisers, mentors, and leaders in extracurricular activities appear to be the most vulnerable to sexual misconduct, particularly if they are very successful, politically connected, and seen as community icons, but at the same time lack training in how to engage in close contact with students. If these successful professionals become involved in sexual misconduct, they are often given a pass by administrators, colleagues, parents, and community leaders with whom they hold long-term allegiances and political connections.

As a result, the failure to confront the problem and the lack of intervention may lead to further misconduct and the adoption of a predatory lifestyle, with the teacher or coaches believing they will not be caught.

Every teacher and coach needs to learn how to carry on close contact with students, many of whom are needy, and how to establish clear boundaries.

Each group in the school—administrators, professional helpers such as guidance counselors, teachers, support staff, students, and parents—need training in how they should respond to teachers and coaches who cross professional boundaries.

There need to be many open doors for help in the school that the victims of sexual misconduct, their parents, and the professionals involved in the misconduct can walk through for help and intervention that can stop the misconduct early on.

Often school districts, teacher unions, and professional associations such as the kind found in athletics are reluctant to offer training to their staff, thinking, "It can't happen here." As a result, sexual misconduct by teachers and coaches is treated as an aberration, a bad seed, rather than one of the many problems that can happen to otherwise successful professionals. The result is that the problem gets little discussion and little or no training resources. It's a dark topic that is off the agenda. We need to raise awareness about sexual misconduct and take it out of the "no-no" column and place it in the column of "it can happen, particularly without training."

Administrators, teachers, support staff, students, parents, and community members are often reluctant to confront teachers and coaches involved in sexual misconduct even when the behavior is obvious and "everyone knows." They fail to trust their judgment and observation skills. They are frozen in denial.

The victims of sexual misconduct are often reluctant to come forward and seek intervention. They feel they will not be believed. They fear they will be blamed by their parents and peers and, in the case of gifted academic or athletic students, may be deprived of scholarships and select college admissions by mentors who are carrying out the sexual misconduct. They become frozen, unable to confront the problem and ask for help.

Teachers and coaches involved in sexual misconduct often fail to come forward and ask for intervention. They feel they will be judged and treated as predators by the school and community. They too remain frozen and without help.

Homosexual and lesbian relationships between teachers and students appear to be underreported and in general not given a place in the training programs for teachers and coaches.

When sexual misconduct does occur, what often follows is a tendency by teachers to pull back from offering help to needy students and close their doors, which results in a school climate of suspicion and rumors rather than offering the needed training for every teacher in how to carry on close contact with students and set clear boundaries. It is a classic case of problem creation in the guise of problem solution.

Outside-of-school activities, such as specialized workshops, camps, tournaments, and classes for gifted academic and athletic students, need to be monitored by school leaders in order to help students avoid coaches and teachers who are at risk for sexual misconduct.

NOTES

1. William Swiggart, Karen Starr, Reid Finlayson, and Anderson Spickard, "Sexual Boundaries and Physicians: Overview and Educational Approach to the Problem," Vanderbilt University Center for Professional Health, 2001, http://mc.vanderbilt.edu/root/vumc/php?site=cph&doc=742.

2. Caroline Hendrie, "In Youth's Tender Emotions Abusers Find Easy Pickings," *Education Week*, December 2, 1998, http://edweek.org/ew/vol-18/14tactic.h18.

3. Andrew Jacobs, "School Official Charged with Molesting Students," *New York Times*, May 22, 1999, 3 (B).

4. David Rhode, "Probation for Teacher Guilty of Abuse at Stuyvesant," *New York Times*, August 19, 1999, 1 (B).

5. Randall C. Archibold, "A Chill at Stuyvesant High," *New York Times*, September 21, 1999, 1, 8 (B).

6. Susan Kaufman, "When Teachers Mix Socially with Students," *News & Observer*, September 29, 1994, 1, 12 (A).

7. Ontario Province Ministry of the Attorney General, "Chapter I: The Nature and Scope of the Review," Review of Kenneth DeLuca Case, 1999, http://www.attorneygeneral.jus.gov.on.ca/english/about/pubs/robins/ch1.asp.

8. Ontario Province Ministry of the Attorney General, "Chapter III: Extent and Nature of Teacher-Student Sexual Misconduct," Review of Kenneth DeLuca case, 1999, http://attorneygeneral.jus.gov.on.ca/English/about/pubs/robins/ch3.asp.

9. Michael Levinson, "Ex-Principal Rejects Naming Honor," *Boston*, December 12, 2004, http://boston.com/news/local/articles/2004/12/ex_principal_rejects_naming_hon.

10. *Southington Journal*, "Town's Disgust Outlasts a Statute of Limitations," *New York Times*, January 14, 2002, 17 (A).

11. Kimberly W. Moy and William Schubert, "Coaches Avoid Charges in Sex Allegations," *Hartford Courant*, January 10, 2002, 7 (A1).

Chapter Five

Training Teachers, Coaches, and Students to Avoid Sexual Misconduct

This "how to" chapter is designed to prepare building administrators to implement a training program so they and their staff are ready to deal with the complex issues involved in sexual misconduct. This training can be best utilized as part of a broad staff development effort to prepare teachers for roles as advocates, advisers, mentors, coaches, and club leaders, roles that bring teachers, coaches, and students together in close, one-on-one, long-term contact.

This chapter fills a gap in the effort to prepare building administrators to deal with sexual misconduct. For example, administrators have been warned about the legal aspects of sexual misconduct, liabilities, and lawsuits, and they have been given information, handouts, and manuals warning teachers, students, and parents about would-be predators.

As researcher Elaine Yaffe points out in her article "Expensive, Illegal, and Wrong: Sexual Harassment in Our Schools,"[1] there is no shortage of published and filmed material designed to help students, teachers, and other staff members become better equipped to deal with these changing times. There are prepared curricula and handbooks containing a wealth of information and definitions of what sexual harassment is, background and summaries of relevant laws, sample policies, instructions on how to conduct an investigation, lesson plans, overheads, first-person accounts of actual incidents, newspaper clippings, quizzes to uncover preconceptions and misinformation, and videos that attempt to give the sense and feel of the problem.

However, while we have given administrators the helpful information that Yaffe suggests, we have failed to provide administrators with a road map on how to train their teachers to deal with close contact with students that can spawn sexual misconduct. The absence of an easily implemented training program has left a glaring gap in our efforts to raise the awareness and competency of administrators when it comes to sexual misconduct preparedness. We have failed to deliver what administrators needed in every case study in this book: training, supervision, monitoring, and intervention.

As a result, we have teachers, coaches, administrators, and even support staff at risk for sexual misconduct. As Frederick N. Brown, associate executive director of the National Association of Elementary School Principals, suggests, turning a blind eye to sexual misconduct is "a career-ending move for a principal. If it's found that you covered up or overlooked something that harmed a child, you might as well pack it in."[2] As mentioned in chapter 3, Old Rochester principal Robert Gardner's protection of John Shockro entailed huge personal and professional costs.[3] He too was Shockro's victim in that he endured the scorn of many community members by acting in partnership with Shockro and was forced to request the removal of a plaque dedicated to his service to the school and the community.

Principal Gardner provides an unfortunate example of what can happen to otherwise caring and competent administrators when sexual misconduct training is not available. Perhaps if Gardner had the training program presented in this chapter, John Shockro might have been helped before he caused harm to vulnerable teens and ruined his own personal and professional life.

Writer Caroline Hendrie suggests that a lack of training leaves many well-intentioned administrators with little understanding of the dynamics of staff-on-student sexual abuse. But her helpful words can never convey the pain and hurt that can come to administrators, teachers, coaches, and student victims when there exists a "lack of training" in our secondary schools.

We need to sell school and community leaders on why it is better to prepare teachers and coaches for the hazards and risks involved in close contact with students rather than leave them at risk and vulnerable to sexual misconduct. In the absence of training and intervention, we should not be surprised when sexual misconduct occurs. The combination of untrained teachers in close contact with needy students is an accident waiting to happen, an accident that comes with great costs to the students involved, their families, the school district, and the community.

As with other successful reform efforts, our first step is to build a support base and make it attractive for teachers and administrators to buy into such training, to see such training as being in their own self-interest, important to their personal and professional development, and having the potential to make them more effective teachers.

In the next section, the focus is on the specific steps needed to train teachers by beginning with an overview of the issues involved in sexual misconduct. A three-part Teacher Sexual Misconduct Awareness Inventory (TSMAI) is then presented, which administrators can use in concert with the training resources of pupil personnel workers such as guidance counselors, athletic directors, teacher leaders, and community mental health resources to raise teachers' awareness about the potential problems involved in close contact with students and how to set boundaries.

However, no training program is foolproof. Clearly marked open doors for intervention need to be put in place to guide teachers and students headed toward sexual misconduct.

In this section, the focus is on how administrators, counselors, social workers, school psychologists, staff, students, support staff, parents, and community members on the front lines of the school can observe educators heading into friendship, love, and sexual relationships with students. Each group will be able to channel observations to administrators who are prepared to provide quick intervention to stop the relationship and direct the educators and students involved to credible sources of help in the school and community.

This section also highlights the important part of listening to "chatter" among students in the hallways, lunchroom, athletic events, and dances and to concerned colleagues and parents. Members of the school community often know when relationships between teachers and students become special and teachers take on risky behaviors, such as taking a student to lunch, giving him or her a ride home, selecting him or her as an athletic assistant, buying gifts, and taking on the role of savior, parent surrogate, friend, or lover.

SELLING THE PROFESSIONAL STAFF, PARENTS, AND COMMUNITY MEMBERS ON THE VALUE OF TRAINING TO AVOID SEXUAL MISCONDUCT

Training teachers to understand the hazards and risks involved in close, long-term relationships with needy and vulnerable students is rarely handled in a proactive way by school administrators, teacher union leaders, and parent/community activists. Rather, it is either considered a taboo subject, one that "can't happen here," or approached solely by giving the professional staff information on the legal aspects of sexual misconduct and implementing a screening process to rid the school of sexual predators.

Screening out predators becomes the focus rather than acknowledging that every teacher, given the right conditions, can be at risk of misconduct. This is a shortsighted remedy at best and, rather than solving the problem, leaves the professional staff vulnerable to sexual misconduct. It is problem creating under the guise of problem solving.

The result is that teachers, teacher advisers, coaches, mentors, and leaders of extracurricular clubs remain at risk of sexual misconduct as they continue to engage students in a variety of helping and supporting roles that are being called for by secondary school reform efforts, such as *Turning Points 2000: Educating Adolescents in the 21st Century*[4] and *Breaking Ranks II: Strategies for Leading High School Reform.*[5]

How do we turn the conversation around and raise the awareness of educators, parents, and community leaders? Before any discussion of training, we need to mount a selling campaign to put the issue of sexual misconduct on the school's agenda. The best approach is to suggest, "Isn't it better, and in the long run more cost effective, to train teachers about the hazards and risks of close contact with students, how to set boundaries, and to recognize the signs of potential misconduct within themselves and their colleagues rather than leave them on their own without the necessary training and skills they need?"

Part of this selling process should emphasize that teachers need a variety of skills to do their work well. And these skills need to cover a variety of different areas that include students' academic and personal development.

We need to ask why school districts provide staff development on issues such as discipline, bullying, inclusion, equity, and so on and leave out training teachers for close contact with students. We can't simply tell teachers to assume a role of advocate, adviser, or mentor with students without providing the necessary training and skill acquisition.

That is a recipe for failure, failure on the part of some teachers because they are unprepared for this new role and naïvely set out in this new role to become saviors, parent surrogates, friends, and, for some, lovers. They are allowed to drift down a path of personal destruction for both teacher and needy teenager.

In the selling process, we need to remind school and community leaders that even if the training and intervention helps only one teacher or coach avoid the path to sexual misconduct, this kind of proactive intervention can save an otherwise successful professional, his or her family, the student involved, and his or her parents from public humiliation and hurt.

We need to remind school and community leaders that there are other costs than the personal one for the teacher, student, and parents directly involved. There are the economic costs. Training may save the district from paying out large sums to victims of sexual misconduct. And there are the costs of the loss of trust in the school district and staff and the damage to a positive school climate that often occur in the aftermath of a case of sexual misconduct.

What often follows is an atmosphere of fear, which includes rumors of alleged misconduct, finger pointing, and teachers closing their doors to close contact with needy students, feeling that they too could become at risk of false allegations.

There is also the cost of community discontent with the district and district leaders, which often results in voting down school budgets and firing administrators. The message in our sales campaign needs to be clear: As leaders in the school district and community, you have a lot to gain by acting and also a lot to lose by not acting. We need to do whatever it takes to avoid putting our professional staff and students in harm's way and avoid destroying the image that the school district is a safe and nurturing place.

The growing need for reforming our secondary schools, as suggested in the *Breaking Ranks II* report, may be just the vehicle needed to help persuade school and community leaders to address the prevention of sexual misconduct. For example, the *Breaking Ranks II* report calls for each student to have a personal adult advocate to help him or her personalize the educational experience, a professional staff member who knows the aspirations, strengths, and weakness of each student and helps him or her become successful in all classes and activities.

The report also recommends that teachers (1) convey a sense of caring to their students so they feel their teachers have a stake in their learning and (2) become adept coaches and facilitators to promote active involvement of students in their own learning.

Requiring teachers to move from a strictly academic focus into the role of personal adult advocate who knows each student well demonstrates a high degree of caring and facilitates the active involvement of each student's needs to include training on how to carry on close contact with students. That means helping teachers move from a lecture-based style of communicating and interacting with students into a facilitating style in which students talk to their teacher/personal advocate about personal, health, and well-being issues that may be negatively impacting their academic success.

For teachers that means learning how to listen, be nonjudgmental, advise, intervene, and help students resolve problems and, as *Breaking Ranks II* suggests, interact with "hard to reach" parents through home visits, Saturday meetings, and meetings outside regular business hours.

Training will be required to bring teachers into the personal adult advocate role model that emphasizes more close, one-on-one, long-term personal contact with students. That training will require attention to the hazards and risks involved in such close contact, developing skills on how to set boundaries with needy students, avoiding becoming a savior, parent surrogate, friend, or lover with a student, and how to seek intervention when signs of a growing personal relationship with a student begin to evolve.

In this way, the issue of sexual misconduct can be addressed quietly as part of a broader staff development effort to ready teachers for more student-centered roles, such as a personal adult advocate, adviser, mentor, coach, or club leader.

In a sense, this approach provides a way for teachers to talk about the issue of sexual misconduct as part of a broader conversation about what takes place when teachers take on new and untried roles, that there are risks and hazards involved, and that it can happen but there are ways to prevent it from happening. In a sense, this is a win-win situation. Not only do we prepare teachers for the roles that will be required in secondary schools in the future, but we also head off future cases of sexual misconduct by connecting this issue to the skills they will need in the future.

This approach also moves the discussion of sexual misconduct into the realm of a potential problem for every teacher and away from the argument that it is only a problem for predator teachers. I believe this approach goes a long way toward helping teachers not be frozen into inaction when they see colleagues or themselves moving beyond acceptable teacher–student boundaries.

Placing the issue of sexual misconduct into a broader training program also has the advantage of removing some of the notoriety and mystique surrounding the topic and reducing anxiety for teachers. This is a far better approach than training that focuses solely on teachers who become involved in sexual misconduct as mainly predators and pedophiles.

For example, Shakeshaft reports that 9.6 percent of students in public schools, some 4.5 million pupils, are likely targets of unwanted sexual attention by a teacher or coach during their school years, suggesting that the scope of the problem appears to far exceed the priest abuse scandal in the Catholic Church.[6]

Training that begins with an approach like this, which suggests there is an epidemic of teacher sexual misconduct that is not unlike the Catholic Church crisis, is doomed from the start. Not only is it anxiety producing for the teachers and administrators involved, but also for students, parents, and community members. Simply put, teachers, like all learners, don't respond to teaching and training that makes them anxious, defensive, unsure, and vulnerable to an anxious student body, parents, and community.

As Michael Pons, a spokesman for the National Education Association (NEA), suggests in his reaction to the Shakeshaft report *Educator Sexual Misconduct: A Synthesis of Existing Literature*,[7] most people, especially parents, will not read the report and understand its nuances. Instead they will hear "one in ten children is abused in school." Alarming students, parents, and staff with statistics, questionable or not, doesn't solve the problem of sexual misconduct; instead it creates other more insidious problems for caring professionals.[8]

Using scare tactics, numbers, horror stories of predators, and, as the educator sexual misconduct report mentioned earlier suggests, creating a coordinator position in each school district to whom "all rumors or allegations or complaints should be channeled" will simply drive caring educators into self-protection mode with the goal of remaining out of the sight and reach of the case coordinator.

As a result, teachers will be more apt to be frozen into inaction rather than becoming a source of intervention, help, and support when they observe a colleague drifting into close relationships with students. It encourages a "not my responsibility or problem" response by teachers. Doors are closed, teachers become wary of close contact, and they will decline to be club leaders, advisers, or chaperones.

Therefore the key to effective training for how teachers and coaches can successfully handle close contact with students and create necessary boundaries lies in giving them the skills required for such relationships. This approach avoids the message that there is an epidemic of sexual misconduct, which often raises anxiety among teachers and coaches and reduces close contact with students. Our work needs to be about removing the mystique surrounding the issue of sexual misconduct, taking it out of the closet, and persuading and training educators that they can prepare themselves to handle this problem just as they learn to handle other student–teacher problems.

In a sense, our training needs to help teachers and coaches develop a protective barrier against falling into sexual misconduct with vulnerable students, not a barrier that prevents caring, helping, supporting, guiding, and sharing hard truths, a barrier that can help them see a red light warning danger ahead and stop efforts to form friendship, a surrogate parent role, and love relations with needy students looking for a caring adult role model in their lives, barriers that set off an alarm when teachers and coaches find themselves needy for emotional contact and turn to their students for such connections.

Clearly educators require ongoing training, skill development, supervision, support from their colleagues, and timely intervention to help them successfully navigate through myriad problems they encounter at different developmental stages in their ever-changing professional careers and personal lives. Avoiding sexual misconduct needs to be given top priority in our ongoing efforts to ready our teachers and coaches for the risks involved in their work.

In the end, this kind of selling campaign to offer teachers and coaches the training they need is directed at challenging some long-held assumptions in our secondary schools, like the following.

Sexual misconduct doesn't happen to teachers who really care about kids. It only happens with sick people.

Teachers don't need to be their brothers' keepers. They are not paid to monitor colleagues' behavior. It is not up to them to act when they see a colleague crossing boundaries. As one teacher told me, "I don't see any of this taking-care-of-each-other nonsense in our contract."

The business of school is teaching students to read, write, do math, and so on. Teachers shouldn't be involved as advisers or mentors or be in close contact with students. That's the job of counselors, social workers, school psychologists, and so on.

Teachers are already too busy dealing with things like testing mandates and standards. They don't have time for training in how to be involved in more personal ways with students.

Sexual misconduct can't happen here. We have some of the most qualified and dedicated teachers in the country. They wouldn't be foolish enough to become sexually involved with a student.

TRAINING TEACHERS AND COACHES TO AVOID SEXUAL MISCONDUCT

After selling teachers and coaches on the need for training and getting them on board the process, the next step is to provide them with an overview of the subtle issues involved in how to avoid sexual misconduct. Creating awareness, as is the case for many efforts of educational reform, is the first and most necessary step in the effort. The best approach to this training may be to include it as part of a broader topic, such as training teachers how to be advisers and personal adult advocates and training coaches about the special issues involved in coaching female and male athletes. This training model can also be used to train teachers, coaches, and religious personnel in community and religious education and athletic programs.

The training can also be utilized to answer the growing need for training priests, ministers, and rabbis on how to handle close contact with their congregation members, including needy children and teenagers. Here is an example of an overview that can be presented in the opening sessions of training to help create teacher awareness about sexual misconduct and to make it real and believable for them.

AN OVERVIEW OF THE ISSUES INVOLVED IN AVOIDING SEXUAL MISCONDUCT

The most successful approach to introduce the training is that it is okay to talk about sexual misconduct. It can happen to any professional in our school district. We are all at risk. Therefore we need to be prepared and know how to respond to such risky behavior if we find ourselves or our colleagues crossing professional boundaries and becoming too involved with students as saviors, friends, surrogate parents, or potential lovers. Everyone can benefit from this training. The key is to create a dialogue among educators that moves the issue of sexual misconduct from the denial stage to reality.

Acknowledge that transference of affection between students and teachers is common in many classrooms and is an important part of the learning process. Students who are cared for and whose contributions are valued tend to be better learners. They are more involved and less likely to offer resistance.

These students begin to feel toward the teacher as they have felt toward other important people in their lives and expect the teacher to deal with them as those important people have or should have done. Teachers who are valued by their students and deemed worthy also tend to be more effective. They are more involved and more apt to risk close contact with their students.

For example, in a caring classroom environment, the personal lives and stories of students become known through daily teacher–student conversations, which encourage close contact. Teachers get to know about their students' parents, siblings, peers, home life, economic status, dreams, hopes, and failures in passing conversations.

And in these conversations the personal lives of teachers also become known to their students, such as the teacher's marital status, children, and home life, outside of school activities, hopes, dreams, and failures. There is a common bond established that suggests that knowing more about our lives will help us establish a classroom learning environment that will enable us to be better students and teachers.

But these kinds of intimate classroom conditions can plant the seeds for sexual misconduct if teachers are not skilled enough to erect clear boundaries and avoid becoming saviors, friends, parent surrogates, and even lovers with their students.

Transference of affection between teachers and students can have a down side when the teacher's own needs for emotional and physical contact are not being met outside the school environment. While transference is a powerful issue in the teacher–student learning process, it is seldom discussed and is not fully understood by administrators and teachers. For example, teachers who are in great need of close emotional and physical contact in their personal lives are at great risk when they become involved in close relationships with students.

These may be needs that have suddenly emerged due to a personal loss such as the death or serious illness of a loved one, needs that may be satisfied by becoming increasingly involved in close contact with students who are themselves needy. These teachers may find themselves naïvely crossing boundaries and, as the saying goes, looking for love in all the wrong places. These can be very successful teachers who become overwhelmed by life's problems and turn to using their close contact with students to meet their personal need for belonging.

Transference of affection to favorite students who are more like us can have its down side. Simply put, liking certain students too much can put one's professional career in peril. We all come into the education profession carrying assets and liabilities from our own backgrounds. Each of us tends to seek out certain types of students, students we are attracted to, feel safe with, and enjoy helping and communicating with. These are the students who may be fun to be around, seek out our help and advice, honor and respect us for our seeming wisdom, and light up when we walk into a room.

These kinds of "special" teacher–student relationships are found in every middle school, junior high, and high school. Look around your school. These kinds of relationships are not hard to find. But they are also red lights that signal possible trouble ahead. Be careful. Proceed with caution.

Transference of affection between teachers and students that focuses on saving the student from personal problems, such as an abusive home life, can trigger involvement in sexual misconduct. Again, each of us comes into the classroom having survived many of life's problems. We've gone down some tough roads. Maybe our parents were divorced, we lost a parent to an early death, we were abandoned, or we grew up in an alcohol- or drug-addicted family environment. We managed to make it out of that risky family environment, often with the help of a caring teacher, and become successful teachers ourselves.

Yet we still remember what it was like being a teenager in that rocky home environment, and when we come in close contact with students dealing with the same problems, we want to help. We want to help them move on to a better world as our teachers helped us. Therefore, because of our own personal experiences as teenagers, we tend to want to help students with certain problems that we too have experienced.

But in the process of helping, sometimes our good intentions get lost in the complexities and pain in our students' lives. We don't see the barriers, the boundaries, and the warning signals. While we do what we can to ease the emotional pain they are going through, it's never enough.

Often the problems our students are experiencing, like ours as a child or teenager, don't go away, don't get better, and in fact get worse. We ignore the signals of danger ahead and slide into the role of parent surrogate, thinking we alone can alter this child's life quickly. We may ignore our best judgment that our role is to do all we can to help this child, but we are not the parents and we can't take this child home at night, even though the emotion we feel says otherwise.

Sexual misconduct can have its beginnings in good intentions, with teachers who because of their own problems as children and teenagers try to save their students from the pain and rough road they travel. In a sense, they move in with the child and become the parent.

No, not in the literal sense, but they begin crossing professional boundaries by remembering their birthdays and special holidays, showing up at their games, checking with other teachers on the students' progress, and offering needed support such as tutoring when needed. All good things, but sometimes these relationships naturally flow into the beginnings of sexual misconduct with the teacher looking to save a needy student and the student looking to be saved, valued, cared for, and thought worthy.

Barriers and signals save lives, whether it is a lighted fence with a warning sign on a winding mountain road or a lighthouse foghorn signaling a treacherous channel ahead. They let us know there is danger ahead and we had best prepare ourselves, be wide awake, vigilant, and responsive. Teachers need barriers and signals when they become involved in close contact with students, barriers that serve as boundaries when they begin heading down a risky road and quickly need a signal, a flashing red light of danger, issuing a jolt that reminds teachers that they have moved into dangerous territory and they had best clear their heads, be vigilant, responsive, and retreat, seeking the counsel of trusted colleagues, administrators, and family members.

The goal of this overview is to point out to teachers that some of the successful practices we employ in the classroom to promote our students' learning and well-being can trigger sexual misconduct if we fail to establish barriers and hear the signal that we are entering a personal relationship that is dangerous. Yes, it is important that we work to create a classroom environment that fosters close relationships between teachers and students. But at the same time, we need to tell teachers that it is important to satisfy their own personal needs for affection outside the school environment and to be aware when they begin to seek out students to meet their emotional and physical needs for contact.

Teachers need to be reminded that the process of selecting certain students as favorites and awarding them special treatment, a process that in my experience is seen as a normal and okay practice in many schools, is actually risky business. It is also risky business for teachers to take on the role of savior and parent surrogate to try to save their students from life's blows, which the teacher may have received as a child or teenager. This is not to say we should not help needy students; far from it. Rather, our helping needs to be focused on being an advocate and harnessing every school and community resource we can to help students move on from their troubled lives.

Sexual misconduct can therefore result from our good intentions to understand and help our students, trying to meet our own personal need for affection and contact through our students, focusing on students we like and are comfortable with, and taking on the roles of savior and parent rather than teacher and helper. In the end, barriers and signals keep teachers stable and focused as they daily negotiate with themselves on how to avoid being a friend, savior, parent, or even lover with their students. Barriers and signals then are the friends of teachers. They remind us that we are human and that our caring can wander off to dangerous places.

We need to keep in mind that while this overview is a valuable first step in helping teachers understand that some of their behavior may trigger sexual misconduct, it probably doesn't lessen their assumption that "it can't happen here." Therefore the next step in the training is to personalize the issue by completing the TSMAI. This inventory can further involve teachers by asking them to reflect on specific questions related to teacher behaviors introduced in the overview.

PREPARING TEACHERS TO COMPLETE THE TEACHER SEXUAL MISCONDUCT AWARENESS INVENTORY

The next step in readying teachers to avoid sexual misconduct is to have them complete the Teacher Sexual Misconduct Awareness Inventory (TSMAI). In leading sexual misconduct training programs, an effective way to begin this phase of the training is to show the films *Mr. Holland's Opus*[9] and *Carried Away*[10] and then proceed to the TSMAI. Both films bring a sense of reality to the training and explore how the personal needs of teachers and students can become entangled in potential or real love affairs.

Teachers in training understand and relate to Mr. Holland. He is a creative teacher with a special gift for caring and involving resistant students. Holland doesn't give up on his students. Rather, he makes himself available and confronts students who are choosing to be passive and not involved. He is a fast learner and is ready to throw out techniques that are failing and risk other approaches. And clearly he is no predator.

But early in his fledgling career Holland encounters a different kind of problem student, showing how vulnerable we are as teachers when we enter close relationships with needy students. Holland's problem is not with disciplining acting out or resistant students. Nor is it a problem that he understands, let alone knows how to solve. Nothing in his graduate teacher education program has prepared him for this event.

The problem is his encounter with Rowena, the female star in the yearly musical he is directing. She is a lonely adolescent and sees in Holland an adult figure that appears to be lacking in her life. She says she has family problems. Yet she is a gifted singer and he wants to help her. She sings "I Need Someone to Watch over Me," and her delivery strongly suggests that "somebody" is Holland. He is flattered by her attention. He is having family problems as well with his wife and deaf son.

A part of him wants a new beginning. His star student says, "Come to New York with me," and a part of him wants to go. But somehow he pulls back. He has the wisdom and skills to sense trouble for himself and for Rowena. He meets her at the bus stop and says, "I can't go." A close call!

He gives us a look into the struggle and the skills needed to not cross boundaries when a part of us says, "Just this once." What are Holland's skills that help him stop becoming involved in sexual misconduct with Rowena?

While at first he does not recognize the danger ahead, he slowly awakens to the risks involved and to the fact that his lonely gifted student with problems wants more and more from him. She wants him to leave his teaching job and his family and be with her in faraway, exciting New York City. He fights off the urge to go and slowly comes to terms with the fact that he has some fence mending to do with his wife and son. His wife senses what is happening. She knows he has been spending more and more time after school with Rowena. She's no fool.

Her intuition tells her that Holland is halfway out the door. In her own way she confronts him and asks him to work with her to save their marriage. He has a built-in barrier and signal that tells him to be careful, there is thin ice ahead. In spite of his personal troubles, he knows that he has a family life and teaching job worth preserving. An important question for teachers once they have viewed *Mr. Holland's Opus* is this: What would you do if an extremely attractive student sought you out as an adult role model, mentor, friend, or father figure?

In *Carried Away*, teacher Joseph Svenden is more vulnerable than Holland and lacks some of his skills to resist temptation. He is no predator. He is a man who thinks slowly and deliberately, but his careful approach is not up to the challenge of resisting a precocious seventeen-year-old student who pursues him. At first he balks at the affair, but eventually succumbs. The affair may be the first reckless impulse he has ever given in to.

Yes, he may have sensed the alarm of danger ahead. But he is too needy for the physical and emotional contact he lacks in his personal life to take a different course. Svenden is swept away. Here are some important questions for teachers after they have viewed *Carried Away*: Do you think teachers like Svenden who do not take care of their own emotional needs are allowing themselves to become at risk of sexual misconduct? What kinds of interventions did Svenden need to help him pull back from crossing boundaries and becoming involved in abusing a vulnerable student? Have you ever found yourself looking to students for affection, contact, and support when personal troubles visit your home and school life?

Reviewing both of these films serves to move the discussion of sexual misconduct from an abstract concept into the reality of what can happen to dedicated and caring teachers when they develop close relationships with students. Completing the TSMAI is the next step in raising teachers' awareness.

THE TEACHER SEXUAL MISCONDUCT AWARENESS INVENTORY: PART I

This inventory will help raise your awareness about the issue of sexual misconduct. Your answers and observations are important, as they will provide material for our discussions. Please try to answer each question.

As teachers, we are all attracted to certain students. For example, these may be students you feel a special closeness to and want to spend more time with. We all have our "favorite" students. Please describe these students and what makes them special in your eyes.

Effective teacher–student relationships go two ways. Teachers as well as students receive something of value from such relationships. What are you getting in return from students to whom you feel close and consider special?

When you were a teenager, was there a teacher whom you felt close to, whom made you feel special, and whom you wanted to spend more time with? Please describe this relationship and any others you have experienced.

Are you attracted to helping students with certain kinds of problems? This might be a student affected by a troubled home life, a divorce or separation, a death or serious illness, alcohol or drug addiction, violence, school failure, poor peer relationships, eating disorders, potential suicide, or physical, emotional, or sexual abuse. Please describe these students and your feelings toward them.

When you were a teenager, did you experience any of these problems in your life? Briefly describe these problems and their impact on your teaching style now.

Do you ever consider taking "problem" students home so they can have a better life, be safe, and be cared for? Have you taken on the role of a parent surrogate by advocating for these students with other teachers, remembering their birthdays, checking on their lives outside of school, even meeting them after school for conferences?

Have there been occasions when you had to draw a clear line, a boundary, between yourself and students who wanted too close a relationship, such as a friend, savior, or surrogate parent? Please describe these situations and what made you sense you might be about to cross a professional boundary.

How did you distance yourself from these students? Did you remain in their lives as a caring teacher and adviser by setting some kind of workable boundary? Or did you find yourself ignoring the students' advances completely?

Did you ever talk, or want to talk, to a colleague, supervisor, friend, or family member about how to avoid becoming too involved in a student's personal life and problems while at the same time being an effective adviser and mentor? Please describe your feelings.

When you observe a fellow teacher becoming too involved with a student, what is your reaction? Do you approach this teacher and share your concern that he or she may be crossing a professional boundary? Or do you consider it none of your business? Please describe your reaction when you observe a teacher beginning to cross professional boundaries and becoming a friend, savior, or surrogate parent to a student.

In most cases of sexual misconduct, colleagues and administrators tend to look the other way when they observe a teacher becoming too involved with a student. Unfortunately this leaves the teacher and student involved on their own and sometimes results in a sexual misconduct relationship that leaves both parties scarred for life. Why do you think colleagues and administrators are hesitant to confront such behavior and direct the teacher and student involved to sources of help before it is too late?

What are your feelings about teachers who cross professional boundaries and become too involved with their students?

Do you think sexual misconduct happens only with male teachers and female students? Do you think female teachers can become involved with male students or that there are homosexual and lesbian relationships that are often underreported?

Can you imagine a situation in which you might become involved in crossing professional boundaries with a student? After all, you are human and have needs for affection. Sometimes our professional guard does come down. Describe a possible scenario in which you might become involved because of your good intentions to help a student.

Whom would you turn to for help and advice if you found yourself heading for a friendship, savior, or parent surrogate role with a student?

Conversely, how would you respond and what would you say if a colleague came to you asking for help and advice on how to separate him- or herself from a deepening personal relationship with a student?

How would you describe "effective professional boundaries" that allow you to become involved in close relationships with students that at the same time offer a barrier, a layer of protection, from becoming too involved?

THE TEACHER SEXUAL MISCONDUCT AWARENESS INVENTORY: PART II

In this second section of the TSMAI, you will be asked to complete three checklists. These checklists will help you develop a greater in-depth awareness about the issues involved in sexual misconduct, such as the student problems that attract our attention, common hazards and risks for teachers involved in close contact with students, and self-controls that help us erect workable boundaries.

Check the student groups and problems you tend to get too involved with.

- ☐ gifted and talented students
- ☐ student athletes
- ☐ male students
- ☐ female students
- ☐ gay and lesbian students
- ☐ students with handicaps
- ☐ average students
- ☐ special education students
- ☐ college-bound students
- ☐ minority students
- ☐ acting out students
- ☐ students who abuse alcohol, drugs, tobacco
- ☐ students returning from rehab
- ☐ students whose parents are separated or divorced
- ☐ students who have experienced the death or serious illness of a family member, friend
- ☐ students who are school failures and potential dropouts
- ☐ students who have health problems such as obesity
- ☐ students who have suicidal thoughts or have made suicide attempts
- ☐ students who have experienced physical, emotional, or sexual abuse
- ☐ students with poor peer relationships
- ☐ students with troubled home relationships

Please check the items that you feel represent hazards and risks for teachers involved in close relationships with students. The teacher

- ☐ holds more than one meeting a week with a certain student. Other students complain that their meeting time is being cut back.
- ☐ switches meetings with the student to late afternoon or evening.
- ☐ begins to hold meetings at a local diner or in the student's home.
- ☐ is flattered by the student's interest in his or her personal life.
- ☐ buys the student presents for birthdays and special events.
- ☐ writes the student letters of encouragement on a regular basis.
- ☐ accompanies the student on field trips.
- ☐ drives the student back and forth to school.
- ☐ spends time with the student at dances and school activities.
- ☐ requests that the student be in his or her class or homeroom.
- ☐ experiences parents who become concerned about the teacher's over-involvement with their child.
- ☐ has other teachers/administrators asking questions about his or her over-involvement with the student.

Teachers can avoid the hazards and risks involved in helping by controlling the where, when, and how of the helping process. Here is a checklist of "Don'ts." Please check any item that might present a hazard for you. Don't

- ☐ drive students to school or home alone.
- ☐ take a student out for a meal.
- ☐ buy a student gifts (birthdays/special occasions).
- ☐ limit your social life to students/school activities.
- ☐ limit your need for an ego boost and flattery to students.
- ☐ hold helping meetings out of school.
- ☐ write personal letters to students regularly.
- ☐ hold helping meetings in late afternoon/evening.
- ☐ short change some students by depriving them of an equal amount of meeting time.
- ☐ mix your helping role with your other roles (homeroom teacher, classroom teacher, chaperone, field trips).
- ☐ neglect to communicate with parents, colleagues, and administrators.

THE TEACHER SEXUAL MISCONDUCT AWARENESS INVENTORY: PART III

Part III of the TSMAI provides examples of how teacher advisers can talk to students about clear boundaries and how teachers and administrators can intervene and help colleagues who are ignoring the hazards and risks involved with students who are asking for friendship, savior, surrogate parent, and even love relationships. The focus of this last part of the TSMAI is to help teachers and administrators consider interventional and confrontational practices and conversations that can address potential sexual misconduct behaviors.

As these examples demonstrate, timely and direct intervention conversations can serve to help teachers define their adviser role with students and spell out the limits of what help they can offer. Timely and direct conversations by teachers and administrators can open a door of help to colleagues crossing boundaries and "teach" them how to pull back from sexual misconduct with vulnerable students.

This kind of intervention conversation not only protects teachers' professional roles, but also presents an opportunity for teacher advisers to serve as a model for "teaching" needy students how to set boundaries themselves as they navigate through teen problems with help from many different adult mentors. Interacting with a teacher or coach who clearly states, "I can offer you support, but I can't be your friend or parent," can bring a heavy dose of reality for teachers and students heading toward a risky relationship.

These types of relationships, as the case studies in this book document, can lead to emotional pain and heartache for students and bring more problems into their already complicated lives. Here are examples of how a teacher adviser can spell out the boundaries and limits for a needy student and how administrators and teachers can talk to colleagues who appear to be ignoring the hazards and risks involved in close contact with students

HOW A TEACHER TALKS TO A STUDENT ABOUT HIS ADVISER ROLE SO BOUNDARIES ARE CLEAR

If a student is looking for a teacher to be a confidant, friend, or surrogate parent who will provide care and nurturing, then teachers need to be able to recognize this process and quickly point out that it is not their role. They need to see it coming and put a stop to it. Divorce, separation, death, or serious illness of a parent can make life appear very treacherous for students, but educators have to draw a clear line at not becoming a friend, savior, or surrogate parents for needy students.

It is important for educators to keep in mind and always remember their mission as professionals is to care and protect students. Yes, there are many students in our schools who need a dad, a mom, loving parents, or someone to save them from life's blows. When loving parents become absent, teachers are often targeted for that role by needy students. However, taking on that role can lead to crossing professional boundaries. Simple words work best for teachers when they try to make their helping role clear and establish professional boundaries. Here is how one teacher approached the issue with a student.

> *I am very concerned about your mom and dad's divorce, but I can't take over their role. I am your adviser, not your parents. I know you don't like going home after school and would rather spend the time talking to me about your problems. But I have my own family obligations after school. I know there are going to be times when a crisis comes up and you need to talk after school. That's okay once in a while, but not on a regular basis.*
>
> *And it's best you don't call me at home. My wife said you called last night. But I do want you to know that I am here to help you. Here is what I can do. I can understand how tough things are and encourage you to keep going, just what I am doing now. I know you're upset about your dad leaving and your mom's depression. I know it's tough. But I also know that continuing to feel sorry for yourself doesn't help you move on with your life.*
>
> *Let's do three things that I think will help. First, your grades. Let's talk about how you can get back to work and not let your grades slip any more. Let's be specific and make a plan. Second, let's get your mom in here and talk to her*

> about getting some help. I know a good social service agency that can help her with emergency food and fuel allowances and legal help.
>
> Third, I know you are free fourth period. I have an extra help class then with some kids who are going through the same thing as you. I know some of these kids call each other at night and try to help. I know the nights can be rough. Getting involved with them might give you additional support and someone to call at night. Why don't you come by?

Here our teacher sets the guidelines for his needy student. He shows he wants to help, but that he can't be a parent. There are definite limits. He indicates that he has his own family responsibilities and calling him at home is not a good thing to do. He suggests an alternative, a fourth period help setting in which other students with similar problems are involved. He keeps his professional boundaries clear. He executes this well.

HOW A VETERAN FEMALE TEACHER WHO IS BECOMING TOO PERSONALLY INVOLVED WITH A STUDENT TALKS ABOUT THE PROBLEM WITH AN ADMINISTRATOR

> *I don't get it. I've never been too involved with any of my students. I've always had a line I never crossed. And I've been teaching for twenty years. I thought I'd seen it all. I'm not some naïve kid just out of grad school. But I find myself spending more and more time trying to help Frank get through the death of his mother. Actually he's handling the death process pretty well. But I can't seem to let him go on his own. I keep inviting him in for conferences and trying to help. All of a sudden it hit me last week.*
>
> *I'm trying to help too much! I'm the one who needs the contact. I'm the one who likes talking to him and looks forward to our meetings. Here I am, a forty-two-year-old woman acting clueless. I also notice that I've been very lonely since my own divorce. When I meet with Frank it just feels good to talk to someone who needs me. I had better do some self-correcting here. Thanks for noticing that I was spending too much time with Frank and inviting me to talk. Sometimes you just don't see things clearly.*

Here the administrator observes a teacher who may be getting too involved with a student. The administrator acts and invites her to talk. The administrator understands that when teachers get involved in too-close relationships with students, it's not just a male phenomenon. Female teachers are also at risk. Another stereotype shot down, denial out and reality in.

Here the administrator provides the teacher with important feedback so she can correct her behavior. If she is left on her own, she may cross over her professional boundaries. Therapeutic supervision requires a response to a teacher at risk. It means not looking the other way, hoping the problem will go away, or thinking, "It can't happen to her. She has twenty years of experience. She's got to know better." Maybe right now she doesn't know better and needs someone to call her attention to it.

HOW A YOUNG, NAÏVE SAVIOR TEACHER HEEDS THE ADVICE OF AN EXPERIENCED COLLEAGUE AND GETS NEEDED HELP FROM AN ADMINISTRATOR

Some teachers tend to help with problems that they have personally experienced. For example, if they have experienced an abusive situation as a child or been involved in an abusive situation as an adult, they sometimes become too involved with a student who is experiencing abuse. These teachers know the emotional pain that goes with abuse and they want to help. Effective teacher helpers learn that personal experiences can sometimes lead to over-involvement with a student who the teacher may perceive as going through the same thing as they did. Professional boundaries must be maintained in spite of the personal experiences and emotional pain of the teacher helper.

Here is how a one-on-one conversation might go on between an administrator and an over-involved teacher who has been confronted by an experienced and caring colleague.

> *It's starting to get to me. All of the kids who have problems with alcoholism in their families keep coming up to my room and talking. At first I thought it was neat. I know how painful it is to have an alcoholic parent. It's something I'll never forget. In fact, that's one of the reasons I went into teaching, to help kids get through these kinds of problems. My tenth grade English teacher, Mr. Mowbray, helped me through my thing.*
>
> *I wanted to be just like him. But a lot of these students, particularly the girls, keep suggesting that I am the only one they can trust and that they never had a real father to talk to about personal things. It's flattering stuff. I even think some of them have a crush on me.*
>
> *I was dancing with one of those students at the junior prom last week and I literally had to tear myself away from her. I felt myself slipping away from my teacher role and getting personally involved. Let's face it, I'm twenty-five and she's seventeen and a knockout. That's only an eight-year difference. It's pretty confusing to me as to where my teacher role ends and a personal relationship begins.*
>
> *I didn't learn anything about this stuff in graduate school. John Proctor, my team teacher, thinks I've gone too far and I ought to pull back. He suggested that I talk to you and get some advice. Has this ever happened to you?*

Here the concerned teacher heeds the advice of a fellow teacher who sees danger ahead. John Proctor's feedback taps into our teacher's own concerns and questions. Proctor's feedback sends the teacher to the administrator looking for help and a way out of this too-close contact. The teacher asks good questions of the administrator. Has this ever happened to you? Where do I draw the line between the role of teacher and personal involvement?

The question sets the focus for the one-on-one conversation. John Proctor throws his colleague a lifeline. His observations and feedback begin an important learning process for our twenty-five-year-old teacher that will hopefully lead to an increased awareness and skills to establish workable professional boundaries. Teachers who care about each other see trouble coming. There are many teachers like our fictitious John Proctor who can act to help a colleague avoid sexual harassment if administrators signal them that this is an important part of their work as a teacher.

HOW A COLLEAGUE CONFRONTS A TEACHER HEADED TOWARD POSSIBLE SEXUAL MISCONDUCT

Effective teachers don't take a student to lunch alone, invite students to their home, regularly write notes to a student, or make regular physical contact. I call these situations *hot spots*. They can get you into trouble. Effective teachers are also more sensitive when they are involved in chaperoning activities such as camping and overnight trips. They know that professional/personal boundaries can sometimes become blurred in these situations.

Here is how a blunt one-on-one conversation goes between a teacher who has experience with how to maintain professional boundaries and an inexperienced teacher who appears to think that helping students can be done only in one-on-one situations away from the school.

> *Dave, you are a good teacher. You've got the potential to be the best in the business. But you've got to stop taking kids out to lunch with you one on one. You are asking for trouble. I know you want to help the kids and that's a great thing. But don't be naïve. When you help, do it in a professional way, in school. I guess I'm trying to be like a big brother to you and suggest there are ways to do things. You can't be every kid's buddy or friend. Like it or not, you are a teacher and you have to act in ways that don't send the wrong message to people.*

> *Look at the other teachers in the building who are good helpers and see what they do. Watch Lorraine Jones and Jim Lowry. They meet with kids in the cafeteria or library. I even see them playing hoops in the after-school recreation program. You'd be surprised how much help you can give kids while playing ball with them. And remember this. If I see you going off in your car*

> *alone with Gina for lunch one more time, you're going to hear from me. I don't want you fired for appearing to be too involved with students like Gina.*

Here a concerned fellow teacher, one with experience and wisdom, intervenes and confronts the clueless teacher who is not avoiding his hot spots. The teacher becomes the big brother and shows the inexperienced teacher how to proceed safely. He suggests that there is danger ahead; watch out. There are many models and options for help. Take a look at them and learn.

The TSMAI can help motivate teachers to talk about their own search for how to set boundaries and establish a protective barrier they can invoke when the teacher–student relationship becomes too intimate. The inventory helps create conditions in which teachers, often for the first time, can voice their concerns about close relationships with students and identify sources of support they can turn to. Here are some examples of teachers' concerns and their search for guidance.

Learning how to set boundaries usually occurs on the teacher's own watch. In most cases, teachers have no training and little supervision on how to proceed. It is a hit-or-miss situation.

Help often comes from a fellow teacher who voluntarily serves as a big brother or sister and models appropriate behavior in close relationships with students.

Many teachers are aware that they have favorite students whom they seek out, but at the same time are bothered by this behavior. They often feel selfish and think that they are depriving other students of needed attention.

Many teachers feel a strong emotional tug to help students with difficult personal problems, but at the same time think they lack skills in the helping process and sense being drawn into unknown, even dangerous territory. Helping students tends to be a confusing role for teachers who lack training.

Teachers are also confused when needy students demand more of their attention; many lack skills in how to say "no" or "I can't." The word "frozen" seems to capture their feelings and behavior.

In terms of sharing thoughts about being attracted to a student, they tend to keep those feelings to themselves or confide in a colleague or friend outside of school. They feel it could be harmful to their career and job security to share their thoughts with an administrator.

They have observed colleagues becoming too involved with students, but generally feel it is not their job to intervene.

Teachers with troubled home lives are often looking for the opportunity to confide in a colleague and share the burden of how these troubles are affecting their teaching performance.

THE IMPORTANCE OF ONGOING SUPERVISION BY ADMINISTRATORS AND PEER OBSERVATIONS AND SUPPORT IN PREVENTING TEACHER SEXUAL MISCONDUCT

The TSMAI results and the discussions that follow highlight the need for ongoing staff development for teachers in how to be effective in the role of adviser, personal adult advocate, coach, and mentor—all helping roles.

They also point out the important voluntary role that colleagues can play in being a mentor, a big brother or sister, in teaching new teachers how to set boundaries, and in confronting experienced teachers when they begin to cross boundaries. It's a powerful role for teachers who, through their own hard-won experience, have mastered the tricky ins and outs of helping students while at the same time knowing how to establish clear boundaries. The TSMAI results also suggest the need for administrators to adopt the role of mentor, a big brother or sister, and use their supervision and observation sessions to create a dialogue with teachers on how to handle close contact with students.

They must engage teachers in issues other than curriculum, discipline, and so on and move the supervision conversation into encouraging teachers to disclose information about their home lives, concerns over connecting with certain students, how to help a student with problems, identifying persons they can turn to for help when they have a problem, and so on.

In other words, they must change the format from a perfunctory session required by the teacher contract into a helping conversation in which the teacher is listened to, guaranteed safety, encouraged to share real concerns, and "taught" by the experienced administrator now serving as a big brother or big sister instead of a boss how to deal with the tricky ins and out that come with teaching needy students.

Administrators who become more closely involved with teachers through supervision sessions in which they model how to carry on effective helping relationships are in a real sense teaching staff members how to handle such relationships with students. Modeling is a critical role in preparing staff. In my book *An Administrator's Guide to Better Teacher Mentoring*,[11] by modeling how to make contact, establish a trusting relationship, set boundaries for what can be discussed, identify referral resources and sources of support for problems that may need more professional attention and are beyond the expertise of the administrator, how to end a helping conversation, and so on, the administrator takes on the role of a mentor who says, "Follow my lead."

Colleagues such as our fictitious team leader John Proctor, described earlier in this chapter, who is a natural ally and is willing to step up to the plate to help a wayward teacher, can also use this kind of modeling. He doesn't look the other way or say "it's not my job" when it comes to intervention. He sees the problem and acts by confronting the teacher and directing him to an administrator whom he respects and who will offer needed supervision and help. Proctor uses simple helping and confronting words that any responsive citizen would employ upon seeing a neighbor or co-worker heading for trouble.

Intervention to help teachers headed toward sexual misconduct is no mystery. It's a two-pronged approach. It requires individual teachers to take notice and have a willingness to confront a colleague. What's important is the contact. It also requires an institutional response, making sure that many doors in the school are open to both the teacher and the vulnerable student. That means expecting administrators and colleagues to observe teacher–student interactions and quickly address any risky behaviors.

And it means guidance counselors, social workers, school psychologists, support staff, students, parents, and community members are expected to keep their eyes open on the front lines of the school and share their concerns when they see teachers and students involved in risky behavior. They are not expected to be rumormongers or vigilantes, but to act as their brothers' or sisters' keepers and not let members of their school community fall through the cracks and become involved in painful affairs that can ruin the lives of both teacher and students.

THE NEED FOR TEACHERS TO PASS ON THE SKILLS LEARNED IN SEXUAL MISCONDUCT TRAINING TO STUDENTS

The awareness and skill acquisition obtained through sexual misconduct training should not be limited to administrators and teachers. Learning how to set boundaries is important not only to protect the teacher's professional role, but also to teach students how best to navigate through life's problems using many different adult resources. Relying on one teacher or adult figure to meet their needs for friendship, help, and affection can lead to more pain and heartache and serve only to bring more problems into their lives in the end.

Administrators do not need a formal training program, a school-wide conference or an assembly featuring nationally known speakers, or handouts and reading materials that present sexual misconduct as an issue of predator teachers who prey on needy students. These activities cause teachers, students, and parents to withdraw from supportive contact and miss the important lesson of how students need to learn boundaries and how to recognize adults they can trust with their problems.

What is needed is to utilize the many open doors of help in the school in which students can join informal, one-on-one, and small-group discussions with a focus on how they can find many sources of help from caring adults in the school and community. This process can subtly point out the hazards of relying solely on one savior teacher or adult to guide them through their teen years. As described in my books *An Educator's Guide to Understanding the Personal Side of Students' Lives*[12] and *Students in Trouble: Schools Can Help before Failure*,[13] there are many venues in most secondary schools for this learning process to occur.

For example, teacher–student adviser conferences; individual and group counseling sessions offered by counselors, social workers, and school psychologists; school nurse–student conversations; training for student peer counseling; conversations between coaches and team members; discipline sessions involving the assistant principal and troubled students; chaperones at school dances and athletic or music events; and the many opportunities for informal conversations between students and caring support staff who are accessible and easy to talk to, such as secretaries in the health, guidance, and administrative offices, hallway and cafeteria monitors, bus drivers, and so on.

These many open doors offer all students from gifted students to potential dropouts the opportunity to learn from a trusted adult how to find the help they need without risk. This kind of process to help students learn about risks in the real world has many parallels in my work in secondary schools as a teacher trainer, student assistance counselor, and guidance counselor. For example, in educating students about the risks of alcohol, drug, and tobacco addiction, I have learned to avoid large conferences and assemblies in which nationally known speakers and reformed addicts address the horrors of addiction. Scare tactics in my view have little impact on students.

Instead what works to increase student awareness is involving them in a variety of helping conversations offered in the venues described earlier, conversations in which they explore why they are using substances, what they are getting out of the experience, how they became involved, and, when they are ready, how they plan to move out of addictive or potentially addictive behavior. This muted approach can also increase student awareness about setting boundaries and how to avoid risky relationships with savior adults. I believe this approach has a greater chance for success than alarming students with horror tales of predator teachers.

Our mission is to help students learn which adults they can turn to and which ones to avoid, not simply limiting their education to identifying and avoiding predator adults. We need to provide them with the necessary skills to assess adults in general, those who can be helpful and those who can harm, as they move on from high school into an adult world in which they will be called on to form many personal and professional relationships. Simply put, high schools need to offer students learning in who they are, their needs, and which adults can be trusted to help them meet their needs and, in the long run, which adults offer the best opportunity for friendship, caring, love, and support. Alarming and scaring students deprives them of exploring these important questions.

The informal self-awareness conversations between caring adults and students in the school need to involve students in looking at their own dark side. That is, how they, like some adults in their lives, ignore the signs of danger ahead in personal relationships and proceed to cross boundaries that lead to pain and hurt by becoming involved in abusive relationships, developing addictions, hanging with acting out peers, and even, like Mr. Holland's gifted student Rowena, trying to forge dangerous liaisons with a teacher seen as a friend, savior, surrogate parent, and lover. Here is a helping conversation that might begin with Rowena talking to the school nurse, whom she trusts.

> *Things have been so bad at my house. My dad is drinking all the time since he lost his job. My mom is working two jobs now and she is never home. The whole thing scares me. This should be the best time of my life. I am a senior, have the lead role in the musical, and my guidance counselor says maybe I can get a scholarship to college. I am attractive and people like me. They say I have a lot going for me. But all I want is out of my house. I am thinking about going to New York and finding an opportunity in a Broadway show. Mr. Holland says he will help me.*
>
> *He has a close friend in New York with an in with some producers. But—this is so hard to say—I want him to come with me. Silly, isn't it? I am only eighteen and he is married and has a grown son. But I think I love him. I have nobody at home, nobody to love. No, we don't have a loving kind of relationship, and I am sure he doesn't know I feel this way. Maybe you can help me get my head on straight.*

This kind of intervention also needs to be offered to the Catherines of the world who fall in love with needy teachers like Joseph Svenden. In *Carried Away*, their relationship is "the talk of the town." Everyone in the school and community seems to know, not unlike the cases of Gwendolyn Hampton, Glenn Harris, and Gary Jarvis described in chapter 2. But no one intervenes. Catherine and Joseph are left on their own while their community observes. However, their story might have been different if a school counselor had chosen to break the silence and act. Here is how the counselor might have intervened. The counselor, Sherri North, begins the session.

> *Thanks for choosing to meet with me, Catherine. My guess is that my request did not come as a surprise. Over the last month you made a number of appointments to see me but canceled each one. Your mother has done the same thing. I want you to know that I appreciate your showing up today. My sense is that this is very difficult for you, but a needed first step. Let me get right to the point. I hope I don't come on too strong, but I feel we need to be honest and not waste time.*
>
> *Here is what I see. You seem to be spending every lunch period and after-school time with Mr. Svenden. I've also seen you riding around town in his*

car. And teachers and parents have told me that you've been at his cabin at the lake. It seems to everyone in the school community that you are having some kind of an intimate relationship with him. I am asking you to tell me what's going on and whether you want my help. What are you trying to find in this relationship?

Catherine is not surprised by Ms. North's comments. She's been wanting to talk to her for months, but hesitated each time. Yes, she is very involved with her teacher, and yes, she knows their relationship is no secret and is dangerous. Her mother knows and has been nagging her to end the relationship and get some psychological help before she goes to the school and blows the whistle on Svenden. She needs to talk to someone and Ms. North is considered the best counselor in the school and would respect her privacy. Catherine responds.

Yes, it's all true. I am involved with Joseph. It just kind of happened. I thought I could bring some joy into his life. He seemed so lonely and has all these home troubles. I try to ignore all the stares from the other kids and the teachers, but lately it's been difficult. Like there's nowhere to hide in this small town. And I worry that he's going to get into trouble because of my affection and lose his job.

That would be just awful because he's a great teacher. The best I've ever had, so dedicated and honest. I blame myself for getting Joseph into all this and I know I should end this thing right now. But every time I make up my mind to tell him it's over, I end up changing my mind. It's like I am frozen and can't speak the words.

So Ms. North sets the stage for an intervention, counseling Catherine in future sessions on how to make a decision about her relationship and then helping her live with her decision. This intervention will involve counseling Catherine's mother and maybe Joseph Svenden once she gains trust in the counseling relationship. Ms. North is on her own in this intervention; other members of the school staff seem to view the affair as a soap opera that spices up the discussions in the faculty room. Many students and parents see the affair as flaunting community morals and values and blame Catherine for instigating the relationship.

They see her as a bad seed out to ruin the professional and personal life of a decent man. No one seems to see Catherine as a victim except Ms. North. She sees Catherine as a confused teen being swept away into a world in which she has no experience. Finally Catherine has a caring adult in her corner, someone who can guide her.

Like an inexperienced teacher seeking guidance from teammate John Proctor, these are examples of how helpful interventions can be offered to a student. A door is opened by a caring school nurse or counselor for a student to tell his or her story and hopefully find an alternative path. Some readers will probably say these student interventions appear too easy to carry out. However, troubled students often respond when they are offered help. Some situations will meet more resistance and tougher words will be needed to wake students up to their dilemma.

For example, words like, "You are asking for trouble. Don't be naïve. This relationship is going to add more heartache to your already troubled life. How much of this emotional baggage do you think you can carry around before you collapse? Look at the numbers. You've missed fifteen days this marking period. You're failing three out of five subjects. You've been late to class thirty times and tardy twenty. You've been referred to the child study team. Your mom has been called to try to explain your behavior. According to the school nurse, you've lost twenty-five pounds in two months. A year ago you were on the honor roll and a happy kid. If this relationship with Mr. Svenden is so great, why do you look so unhappy and seem to be literally falling apart? You've got a serious problem that needs to be worked on beginning right now. As the school psychologist, I know about kids having troubles and I know how to begin helping them."

However, not every offer to help is met with a positive response by students. The response, "No, I don't have a problem and no, I don't need your help" can also be expected. But such offers serve as a beginning step in intervention. This initial helping conversation unmasks the problem, takes students out of denial, causes them to think seriously about their plight, and shows them where they can turn for help when they are ready.

Teaching students how to learn to set boundaries with peers, romantic relations, parents, teachers, coaches, and significant adults in their lives can also be done in small groups facilitated by counselors, social workers, and school psychologists, as well as being part of training students to be peer counselors. Boundary setting can also be taught as part of the curriculum in health and English classes. For example, in health class students learn positive behaviors and how to seek out reliable adult role models. In English class, they learn from literature how teens and adults face their own dark sides and avoid being lured into damaging relationships.

In fact, teaching students about boundaries and how to form healthy relationships is finally becoming a part of the national discussion on how to prepare students for the personal aspects of teen and adult life. Over the past thirty years, academics have been developing the study of "close relationships," forming the International Association for Relationship Research to share resources and data.[14] Such research is "not just about what makes people happy but how relationships can affect other things, for example, someone's health," says Lisa Baker, assistant professor of psychology at Purchase College, part of the State University of New York.

According to Baker, in recent years some professors have moved beyond theory, making the discussion more personal by teaching relationship skills they can use outside the classroom. Lecture topics and workshops offered at an increasing number of colleges and universities include "Falling in Love without Losing Your Mind" and "How to Break Up without Falling Apart." The latter class includes discussions on how to end a relationship cleanly. As Baker reports, some academics question whether classes like these belong in the college setting, but others say there is no reason love should be ignored.

Teenagers should be offered the same kind of learning opportunities on how to form healthy relationships and end those that bring harm, abuse, and isolation. Having students learn about relationships in secondary school can help them avoid potential pitfalls as they navigate the many problems of teen life. They shouldn't have to wait until college for such training or, for students going directly into the workplace, receive no training at all. Yet secondary schools are increasingly busy places with many mandates. Arguing to set up additional courses in relationship building would draw instant resistance from administrators and teachers already hard-pressed for resources and time.

Relationship-building skills that include learning to set boundaries, form healthy relationships, and end destructive ones can be easily added to the many existing helping and curriculum venues I described earlier and serve to help the Rowenas and Catherines in our schools avoid the hazards and risks that ill-advised love relationships can bring. Waiting to offer students such training can create a climate for sexual misconduct, with smitten students involved with needy teachers and lacking the skills and know-how to avoid or end such relationships, frozen and not knowing how to say no.

In conclusion, teacher sexual misconduct is more apt to happen when teachers and students lack this kind of supervision, peer support, and commitment by the entire school community to act as their brothers' or sisters' keepers. Effective teachers need an ongoing support network to which they can turn for help with professional and personal problems. Each secondary school needs clear, well-lit, open doors for help, the kinds of help available for myriad problems, not simply those related to academic teaching.

No professional life is without trouble or trying times. Good teaching years can be followed by a year or years filled with failure. What works one year for students fails the next year. While teaching careers are sometimes described as one steady experience, the reality is that there are many ups and downs. Teachers' obituaries tend to be the same: "John Franklin taught history at Worcester North High School for thirty-three years." But for most teachers, each year in their teaching career is different.

The best of us can come across situations in which we begin to doubt our competency and skill. And no area is more difficult to exit than becoming too personally involved with a student. It puts teachers in a double bind. They desperately need to talk about the problem, but they are afraid, sometimes justifiably, that if they ask for help they will be labeled as a teacher who is over the line, out of control, often for the rest of their career. It is not easy for students or teachers to move beyond a negative label.

Caring administrators and colleagues like John Proctor can offer these troubled teachers the beginning help they need, not, as is often the practice, leave them be, alone, isolated, and labeled as a bad apple that the administration and community would like to see vanish. The caring, sometimes blunt feedback from the John Proctors of the world starts the healing process and offers the opportunity to plan how to separate oneself from over-involvement.

An important component of training, therefore, is to have teachers identify people in their support network who will help if needed and not turn them away. If they can't list anyone, which is not unusual, then training needs to help them learn how to enlist such support. The training also needs to ask teachers to identify the colleagues they help on a regular basis. This process helps remind teachers that they need to serve as their brothers' or sisters' keepers and not let one colleague fall through the cracks. We do have a responsibility to guard the welfare of colleagues as well as students and parents.

In the end, each of us as educators can at some point in our careers become at risk. We need caring, skilled administrators and colleagues in our corners to help us find our way. And we need to pass on our training in sexual misconduct so students also learn how to set boundaries, form healthy relationships, and end destructive ones. They too need to be prepared for the complexities that come with close relationships.

However, as we see in chapter 6, the goal to provide more training and intervention to reduce sexual misconduct in the schools has not been realized by 2016. In fact, the goal to reduce sexual misconduct has been sidelined by powerful and well-financed school reform efforts that have overwhelmed administrators, teachers, support staff, parents, and, most important, students.

Reforms that have used, some say abused, financial and time resources of local schools needed to help students resolve their personal, academic, and well-being problems. However, change may be on the way to recapture the primary mission of the public schools to be places where students are cared for, helped, and able to find their way to be successful.

NOTES

1. Elaine Yaffe, "Expensive, Illegal, and Wrong: Sexual Harassment in Our Schools," *Phi Delta Kappa* (special report, November 1995): 37.

2. Caroline Hendrie, "Cost Is High When Schools Ignore Abuse," *Education Week*, December 9, 1998, http://www.edweek.org/ew/vol-18/15handle.h18.

3. Michael Levinson, "Ex-Principal Rejects Naming Honor," *Boston*, December 12, 2004, http://boston.com/news/local/articles/2004/12/ex_principal_rejects_naming_hon.

4. Anthony W. Jackson and Gayle A. Davis, *Turning Points 2000: Educating Adolescents in the 21st Century* (New York: Teachers College Press, 2000), 140–44.

5. National Association of Secondary School Principals (NASSP), *Executive Summary of Breaking Ranks II: Strategies for Leading High School Reform* (Reston, VA: National Association of Secondary School Principals, 2004), 1–6.

6. Caroline Hendrie, "Sexual Abuse by Educators Is Scrutinized," *Education Week*, March 10, 2004, http://www.edweek.org/ew/ewstory.cfmlug=26Abuse.h23.

7. Caroline Hendrie, "Preventing Sexual Misconduct," *Education Week*, March 10, 2004, http://www.edweek.org/ew/ewstory.cfm?slug=26Abuse-B1.h23&keywords=sexual%20ab.

8. Caroline Hendrie, "Report Examining Sexual Misconduct Taps Some Nerves," *Education Week*, July 14, 2004, http://www.edweek.org/ew/ew_printstory.cfm?slug=42Abuse.h23.

9. ChucksConnection Film Review, "Mr. Holland's Opus," http://www.chucksconnection.com/holland.html.

10. Fine Line Features Synopsis, "Carried Away," http://finelinefeatures.com/carried/synopsis.htm.

11. William L. Fibkins, *An Administrator's Guide to Better Teacher Mentoring* (Lanham, MD: Scarecrow Press, 2002), 173.

12. William L. Fibkins, *An Educator's Guide to Understanding the Personal Side of Their Students' Lives* (Lanham, MD: Scarecrow Press, 2004), 245.

13. William L. Fibkins, *Students in Trouble: Schools Can Help before Failure* (Lanham, MD: Scarecrow Press, 2005), 91–161.

14. Martha Irvine, "Colleges Offer Classes on Relationships," Yahoo!News, February 13, 2005, http://yahoo.com/news?tmpl=story&cid=514&u=ap/20050213/ap_on_re_us/teaching.

II

Since 2006 Many Schools Have Abandoned Their Mission to Protect Students

Chapter Six

A Perfect Storm Brings a New Wave of Sexual Misconduct to the Schools

A perfect storm allowing sexual misconduct to increase in our secondary schools has emerged since the publication of the first edition of this book in 2006. What should have been a wakeup call to schools calling for increased vigilance to observe and report sexual misconduct and the development of intervention programs to address the problem and offer counseling for students, parents, and staff has not become a priority in many of our secondary schools.

Nor has training for staff members on how to avoid sexual misconduct and come to the aid of colleagues who may find they are crossing boundaries and becoming involved with needy students as friends, parent substitutes, and even lovers become a priority. Rather, the daily lives of many administrators, counselors, teachers, and support staff have become consumed by the increase in reform efforts and testing and a lack of up-to-date intervention system that could serve to prevent the cost of sexual misconduct to needy students and staff.

At-risk staff members and at-risk students make for risky partners, and often their beginning liaisons can be easily observed by caring teachers, support staff, administrators, and parents. However, as this second edition suggests, our large secondary schools have become institutions in which staff are too busy and overwhelmed to care and view their role as a protector of both students and staff heading toward sexual misconduct.

As a result, many educators look the other way as ill-fated student–staff liaisons develop. Some of these staff members are messiah figures who seek out at-risk students for their own sexual pleasures. However, many staff members involved are at risk themselves, needy individuals who find themselves looking for relationships and comfort due to home problems such as a divorce, death, addiction, and ill health.

They are not perverts that need to be shown the door, but often successful teachers who have lost their way and need intervention to help them see they are crossing boundaries and need to develop a red light of danger ahead in close relationships with students. They need training to help them navigate through the risk of too much contact with needy students. But in most schools, no such training exists, except on faded paper in a never published staff training proposal.

One must remember that in our present culture, many teens are sexually active and come to school wearing sexually attractive clothing. Hormones are in the air. It's not the 1950s anymore, when strict student dress codes warned students to keep their bodies hidden. Many of these students, both female and male, are attracted to female and male teachers and coaches whom they see as comforting adult figures that they can confide in and will provide them with a sense of safety, acceptance, and security that is absent in their home lives.

It is also important to remember that misconduct is carried out by both male and female educators in heterosexual and homosexual/lesbian relations. It's not just a male educator having a relationship with a female student. In today's world, middle schools, junior high schools, and high schools are sexual hotbeds. Educators who have close relations with needy, attractive students can find themselves involved in sexual misconduct without having the necessary training to guide them through the risky aspects of such relationships. To do otherwise is to ask for trouble, big trouble.

Many of our schools have become institutions that can be described as "too busy to care," which begs the question, "Is anyone listening to the kids?" We are hatching a new breed of educators who now work and live a world in which all that matters is implementing successful reform and gaining high test scores and who say, "There is no time left in my day to be anything more."

These are school organizations in which educators are silently given a bye to let the emotional needs of teens go unaddressed. Many of these educators were once caring individuals, but they have become steeled against dealing with problems outside their sphere of concern, responsibility, and job demands. They have been forced into becoming technocrats focused on numbers to make their school "look" successful, rather than on being caring and protective educators focused on the lives of students, parents, and colleagues and knowing each of them well.

As a result, increasingly in our schools many troubled teens go without needed intervention except from troubled, at-risk, and savior educators who have a pattern of crossing professional boundaries and luring these needy students into sexual misconduct. For example, because of the increasing mobility of families and the related problems of illegal immigration, unemployment of family members, low paid jobs, and lack of family time together, more teens are on their own and at risk to problematic behaviors. Those teens can be labeled "at risk," be star performers, or gifted athletes who form too close relationships with their coaches and teachers in the search for college admissions and scholarships.

Every student in the school as well as every educator can be "at risk" and heading toward the margins of school life, not just those students who live in poverty and broken homes. More children and teens are coming to school with personal, well-being, and health problems and finding our schools ill-prepared to help them. This is a combination of educators being too busy to care and students needing too much care and has made for a combustible mix in our schools.

For example, teachers are fleeing Arizona in droves, resulting in a serious shortage of experienced teachers. State officials are warning of serious consequences if the exodus continues. Over the last five years, thousands of teachers have left the state, according to a 2015 report by the Arizona Department of Education.[1]

Why are so many teachers leaving? Low pay, insufficient classroom resources, and so many testing requirements and teaching guidelines that educators feel they have no instructional time and flexibility in their own classroom.

In the Miami Unified School District, east of Phoenix, the superintendent is also a grant writer and the principal of the elementary school is also in charge of keeping toilets running as the director of maintenance. "We've asked our teachers to double up, everyone is doubling up," said Sherry Dorathy, the superintendent of the district.

Andrew Morrill, the president of the Arizona Education Association, told CBS 5 in Phoenix that along with low education spending and low salaries, teachers feel under siege by so many testing and instructional guidelines.

The education world has become so busy with handling an unparalleled number of demands for change that often educators forget that the world our students occupy is under siege. And the siege has a different impact for many families. For example, many parents are out of work or working in low-paying jobs that require their family to exist below the poverty line, live in unsafe and rundown housing, and have no access to childcare, pre-K schooling, and easily accessible health and mental health care.

They are trapped in a survival mode in which school failure and poor health and mental health reign. These are parents and their children that have no clout in the schools, often labeled "at risk" and headed toward failure and the margins of school life. The middle class in the United States continues to shrink and upward mobility is a thing of the past for many Americans.

And then there are families who enjoy living in a world in which they are successful and their everyday needs are easily met. They live in comfortable and safe upscale housing with neighbors like them, are busy leading community and school parent activities, have connections to excellent health, mental health, and recreation resources, tutoring and coaching opportunities for their children so they are successful in sports and school, and have the skills and know-how to manipulate their schools into providing their children with the best teachers and coaches and opening up doors to the best colleges and universities.

They are parents who have clout and are not afraid to use it and push their children to be the best and brightest. But often their children lead lonely personal lives and struggle to keep up the role of being the best and brightest student and looking for relief and a shoulder to lean and cry on.

Often both types of families spawn needy children who can be at risk for sexual liaisons with troubled educators acting as saviors, friends, and surrogate parents. Loneliness and lack of acceptance impact students from every corner of the school community, but too often educators in the past have associated sexual misconduct only with students from so-called broken and impoverished homes.

However, being needy is often a condition well known to many students at some point in their school life. It's a gnawing feeling of emptiness that can lead students into mischief and trouble trying to find relationships in all the wrong places, like a bad sore that never heals.

The following chapters will tell the story of how this perfect storm has come about in our schools, why problems such as sexual misconduct are being allowed to spread, and what can be done to return our schools to "schools that care and protect students" and educators "who care, protect, listen, and act when their students become involved in harmful, abusive relations such as sexual misconduct."

NOTE

1. Valerie Strauss, "Why Teachers Are Fleeing Arizona in Droves," *Washington Post*, June 19, 2015, http://www.washingtonpost.com/blogs/answer-sheet/wp/2015/06/19.

Chapter Seven

The Tragic Stories of the Lives of Students and Educators Involved in Sexual Misconduct Are Being Hidden behind a Wall of Cold, Impersonal Data

Jane Meredith Adams[1] suggests that the failure of U.S. schools to protect students from sexual abuse by school personnel is a story of district cover-ups, lack of training, incomplete teacher background checks, and little guidance from the U.S. Department of Education.

Adams says that the U.S. Government Office reports an estimated 9.6 percent of students, nearly one in ten, are subjected to sexual misconduct by teachers, coaches, principals, bus drivers, and other school personnel during their K–12 career. Adam says the figure is from a 2004 report made by the U.S. Department of Education and is the most recent estimate available.

Adams suggests that part of the problem is lack of required training for school district employees. For example, under California law, employees are mandated reporters of possible child abuse and must immediately notify law enforcement or child protective services of their suspicions, but they are not required to take part in training in the nuances of recognizing abuse and specifically how to spot and report inappropriate behavior between school employees and students and the importance of boundary settings for staff.

Usually a lack of important training to help staff learn the nuts and bolts of how to avoid too close and intimate contact with needy students gets lost amid the many demands like meeting the demands of reforms such as Common Core now facing administrators and staff. It's a case of leadership in our schools being too overwhelmed and forced into a benign role of looking the other way to a growing problem that results in creating an opening for needy students and staff to cross boundaries and become friends and parent substitutes when they should be protecting our children.

It's ironic that education leaders can mandate reform efforts, but look the other way when our students are in danger of sexual misconduct. Without the necessary mandated training and ongoing supervision for staff, schools are tacitly giving permission to not only needy teachers and coaches starting liaisons with students, but also to messiah teachers who are perverts and use their manipulative skills to lure the innocent into sexual relations.

In many schools, it's a story of school leaders abandoning their pledge to protect every student from harm. Without required training and close supervision, the gates to sexual misconduct are left wide open and there is no one around to provide the necessary intervention required. Many educators are too busy reforming, pushing for high scores, getting the best and brightest student into elite colleges, and pampering gifted students and their ambitious, aggressive, do-for-me parents to notice and act to stop the cases of misconduct that are taking place before their very eyes.

But that's exactly the scenario in today's "too busy to care" schools. Administrators and staff are overwhelmed with reform efforts, testing, and promoting their school as a success. As a result, there is one more layer added to the growing perfect storm that is ruining our schools and creating a school culture that many staff and administrators view as more and more nonessential tasks being forced upon their core education duties and ruining their professional and sometimes personal lives, shattering their dream of why they became educators; to help, educate, care, and protect students as they were helped as students.

The rise of sexual misconduct is often at the tip of the iceberg when schools become places in which staffs have become too busy to care, have closed their doors and are isolated, and nobody is watching or listening. And where there is darkness, mischief and trouble find their place and hurt and despair looms where care was once a priority.

However, it must be said that even though the powerful forces of reform have paralyzed efforts of school leaders to provide care, protection, and intervention for all their students, the blame for the rise of sexual misconduct ultimately resides with school leaders. One must raise the questions: Could the school leaders have done more to stop the rise of sexual misconduct by providing training, supervision, monitoring, and intervention when needed for staff? Did they fight hard enough to make sure budgets for training and intervention were to remain "untouchable" and not negotiable? Or in the pursuit to get along did they settle to be partners with reformers and choose to look the other way when at-risk students needed intervention? Or was it safer politically for them to focus on increasing academic achievement rather than training staff to avoid sexual misconduct and empowering teachers on the frontlines to act as first responders when evidence of too-close contact between educators and students emerges?

As a result, more and more educators are being left on their own. Not knowing how to set boundaries, ignoring the glowing red light of danger, ruins many lives and has its terrible cost. Liaisons between students and educators are often known by peers, the administration, support staff, students, and parents. It's happening before their eyes that have become been darkened and their ears blocked to the calls of needy students and staff for help.

When they say "I am not trained how to observe and intervene," they are right. They know they lack the confidence, tools, and skills required. After all, they were trained to be "academic" teachers, not advisers, mentors, or advocates. When many educators say it's "not my job," it is an honest response because not only are they not trained, but school leaders also have not sold them on a new role: intervening when they observe students and staff becoming involved in risky behaviors.

As a result, the hard truth about sexual misconduct is that many observers who might have intervened or at least reported the blooming affair often look the other way, say it's not their job to get involved or they are too busy, close their doors to the tragedy that is taking place before their eyes, in their school, and on their turf. It's an evil force that has entered their school and has left them paralyzed, unable to intervene and help those afflicted by this evil spirit.

This is a demoralizing condition in schools in which many caring educators serving on the frontlines could be making a huge difference to care and protect students if only training was offered to them and they were encouraged to take on the important roles of protector and adviser.

Meanwhile, the student–educator sexual relationship often grows more complicated. Secrets are hard to keep. What everyone knows and kept secret often becomes public knowledge at some point. In the end, the participants involved, the student, his or her parents, the staff member, his or her family and colleagues, and the reputation of the school and administration all come under attack for not doing enough to prevent this kind of sexual misconduct. But it's too late. The damage has been done.

Damage that could have been prevented early on if mandated training was required for staff and if a concerned peer, administrator, support staff, student, parent, or citizen had spoken up and demanded an inquiry. Spoken up in order to stop the damage early so the student did not have to endure the shame of his or her act and dismissing pervert teachers before they do the same abuse to another student.

We need to have mandated training programs for staff that highlight real stories of what can happen to needy students and educators when they cross boundaries, not just statistics about the numbers of students and staff involved. Statistics, data, and numbers don't tell the real stories about what can happen when needy students and staff members find themselves attracted to each other.

Data such as the number of sexual misconduct cases per year do not reveal the real tragedy and despair felt by students and educators and as such can be easily dismissed by educators as simply data that is impersonal, distant, and has little grip on their lives and thinking.

What we need are real stories that staff members can identify in both a professional and personal way. Stories that can get their attention and help place them in a position in which they can understand just how easy it is to become involved in a too-close relationship with a needy student. Stories that demystify the cries of many educators, parents, and citizens that "this kind of thing can't happen here" and, for educators, "that this kind of behavior would never happen to me."

Sexual misconduct can happen to any staff member and any students involved in close personal relationships such as clubs, sports, advisers, field trips, outside the school tutoring, and so on. This is not to say that educators should avoid close contact with students and give up their important mission to know them well, but rather to strongly remind them that there are issues they must be aware of and make sure when they find themselves crossing boundaries that they have a support group of caring peers to turn to, not go it alone and hide their real dilemma and mixed feelings. Educators tell students it's okay to ask for help. The same needs to be true for educators.

However, in our busy schools, mandated training to better prepare staff how to avoid sexual misconduct and how to intervene when they observe a colleague headed for misconduct is not the norm. Rather, schools, if they do any training at all, often focus solely on data about misconduct and identify pervert/messiah staff members as being the main culprit rather than naïve, needy, staff.

This kind of training is focused on pervert staff members and leaves needy teachers vulnerable to sexual misconduct out of the loop and out of the discussion. It lacks any focus on the key point that sexual misconduct could happen in their school and to them. They are human, not made of steel, and as such vulnerable to temptation. Unfortunately, the training is never about the staff members in the school, but rather about data supporting the argument that perverts are the ones to watch and beware of. The message is that good guys and gals on the staff don't stoop to such banal behavior. They are above feeling lonely and needy or so they think (falsely, that is).

The kind of short-sighted training is all about the other guy or gal from some other place who is a skilled, manipulative, evil pervert out to seduce and harm naïve and innocent students. It rarely focuses on the concerns of local staff and their own need for training and supervision in how to be involved with close and intimate contact with students, rather than on the national problem of sexual misconduct lead by pervert educators.

An "it can't happen here" training day doesn't get close to giving staff the tools they need to understand that temptation, loneliness, and being needy are human conditions that can drive many educators to forget their role, risk their job, and do dangerous, risky things. In fact, it's no easy task to stay focused on one's mature adult role when the opportunity for comfort and contact comes knocking hard on one's classroom door, wants to come in, and won't go away. Educators may be best served not to malign colleagues who become involved in sexual misconduct because someday they may be facing the same dilemma.

A focus solely on sexual perverts as the main cause of sexual misconduct is in the end a training that is a quick fix and does little to engage staff in a dialogue about their own vulnerability to sexual misconduct, how they handle close and intimate contact with students, and what kind of a support they can turn to when they begin finding themselves avoiding the red light of danger ahead.

Educators often put up walls of silence when it comes to a closer look at their vulnerability and risk of sexual misconduct, but it is the only way to better prepare them to be aware that they are human and having a strong will and pledging to always do good may not prevent them from succumbing to an attractive student who sees them as a friend, parent substitute, or even a lover. Educators like to be liked by their students and sometimes they require more personal contact from their students than is appropriate.

But this kind of training and related supervision model rarely happens in schools that have become too busy to care. After all, isn't it easier and safer for educators to talk about cases and data about sexual perverts as the major cause of sexual misconduct rather than their own vulnerability to such behaviors? It's an old story. Let's keep talking and focus on sexual perverts from some far away school and keep our own staff risk and vulnerabilities at bay.

The next chapter provides an example of why in-depth training focused on the risks involved for educators in close and intimate contact with needy students, the skills needed to successfully navigate through the perils of such contact, and why these close contacts and relationships are very much needed to better know and help at-risk and lonely students. This is a training that focuses on the need of caring and well-trained educators to connect with needy students, not turn them away and close the door to the academic, personal, and well-being help they need. This is an intervention model that can challenge the present power and role of reformers and test fanatics and demonstrate that our schools can once again be places that care for and protect their students and teachers can once again have time to know their students well and carry out their dual roles of being both academic teachers and meeting their personal health and well-being needs.

NOTE

1. Jane Meredith Adams, "Schools Failing to Protect Students from Sexual Abuse by School Personnel, Federal Report Says," *EdSource*, February 8, 2014, 1–6, http://edsource.org/2014/schools-failing-to-protect-students-from-sexual-abuse-by-school-personnel-federal-report-says/57023#.VUeghyFviko.

Chapter Eight

A Case Study of What Administrators Should Not Do When a Potential Sexual Misconduct Issue Emerges

This is a real story that tells the tragic tale of what can happen to a successful teacher and how the fallout of this sad tale had negative percussions not only for the student and teacher involved, but also for the school and district administrators. The main character is not a pervert. She is a teacher in a large suburban high school who is left on her own to figure out what has become a tragic life; becoming involved in sexual misconduct in which the victim is male a high school student.

And it seems that everyone knows, including the administration, district office, staff, support staff, and parents, but she drifts alone, not able to give up the relationship but knowing she is doomed, wondering why no one comes to her rescue and offers tough love for her to change before it becomes too late. It's a tale of a perfect storm in which the boat plows naïvely into a terrible storm instead of retreating to its safe port. Danielle Watkins, the thirty-two-year-old Stamford Connecticut High English teacher, was in a similar situation.

She was aware of the great danger ahead but continued on crossing professional boundaries with no flashing red light to warn her to stop. In the end, Watkins was arrested. Here's an overview of how things went wrong.[1]

The best of teachers can go over the edge, cross boundaries, and slip into sexual misconduct if no one is watching, caring, or willing to intervene. These teachers like Watkins do not start out as predators only interested in seducing innocent victims. Rather, they are excellent teachers until one day something clicks and they become involved in sexual misconduct with a vulnerable student, like Watkins, who made her student victim meet her own sexual needs and controlled his life by offering him sex and drugs.

In Watkins's case, she was a successful thirty-two-year-old teacher, but in 2013 she started a relationship with one of her male students. The two had sex regularly and exchanged naked photos until the student came forward and reported the sex abuse. According to the Stamford police, Watkins threatened to fail him if he did not continue their sexual relationship. The police also found that Watkins sent the teen thousands of text messages and naked photos.

She also supplied the student with marijuana. Watkins pleaded not guilty to the charges and was placed on leave. Despite Stamford Public School staff members having suspicions about Watkins as early as February 2013, she was not reported to authorities until June 23, 2014, the last day of school.

But Watkins's story involves more than the affair. It involves administrators at Stamford High School and the district office. The police believe Stamford High School's principal, Donna Valentine, and its assistant principal, Roth Nordin, learned about the affair six months before the eighteen-year-old victim came forward and never told anyone. The two conducted their own secret investigation but never notified police. It was not clear what the two found during their investigation or what, if any, punishment they ordered.

Valentine and Nordin were criminally charged and will be fired pending a school board vote and Assistant Superintendent Michael Fernandez will resign from his post. Stephen Falcone, the district's human resources director, will be suspended for four weeks and two Stamford High School security guards and a social worker are also being disciplined.

So it appears those in leadership positions had a good idea that Watkins and the teen were having a sexual relationship, but the district appeared to put up a wall of secrecy to protect the district and mounted a plan of resistance that stressed "this kind of sexual behavior between staff and students doesn't happen here. This is Stamford High School, an excellent institution with a fine reputation, a reputation that needs to be preserved. Let the staff members have their suspicions. Time may be in our side."

It seems that the plan of the district leaders was to go slow, keep the concerns secret among the leadership team, inform those in sensitive positions in the school to keep quiet, and hope that this would all go away. Maybe the thinking of the school and district leadership was "if we make it to graduation day on June 23, it will all be behind us. The teen will graduate and be on his way. We'll deal with Watkins in due time."

So it appears deals were made to keep the lid on the misconduct. Fernandez and Falcone were told of the case by Valentine after she had Watkins placed under surveillance for at least two months. But Fernandez, after consulting with the board's lawyers, advised her to get statements from the people at the school who had seen or heard things that caused their suspicions about the teacher.

The statements were taken and given to Fernandez and Falcone, who also failed to alert state child protective services or law enforcement to the suspicions. They told investigators they also did not bring the suspected misconduct to the attention of school superintendent Winifred Hamilton.

In addition to the administrators, two security guards received letters of warning for their participation in Valentine's month-long surveillance of Watkins without reporting the case to the authorities. Stamford High School social worker James Cooney also received a warning.

Investigators said Cooney had been made aware of the suspicions that Watkins was having sex with a student during conversations with Assistant Principal Angela Thomas-Graves in the spring of 2014. According to Cooney, Thomas-Graves informed him of the rumors, saying that she heard them and notified Nordin.

Valentine and Nordin were arrested on October 2, 2014, and charged with failing to alert the proper authorities under the state's so-called mandated reporter law.

It is clear many folks were aware that Watkins was crossing boundaries and was troubled and in trouble. She was an at-risk teacher who needed intervention. Her teen lover was also an at-risk student and needed intervention. Their drama was becoming more intense, with Watkins threatening to fail the teen if he cut off their relationship. She was becoming more desperate, perhaps due to having to face the relationship was ending.

Meanwhile, the supposedly skilled leadership at Stamford, besides Superintendent Winifred Hamilton, were busy holding the suspicions of many staff members close to their vests. Hiding may be a better word. In the meantime, Watkins was left to her own devices, growing more and more anxious, sending the teen naked pictures, getting him marijuana, and threatening to fail him if he wanted out. It appears they were more interested in saving their school's reputation and praising the banner "Stamford High School Says No to Sexual Misconduct."

It appears no one came to Watkins's aid. She was left swinging in the wind, isolated, and growing more aware that her relationship with the student was soon to be over. It appears that no one came to the aid of the teen until he spoke up about the affair with the support of his parents or friends.

Also left on their own were those staff members who knew that Watkins was involved in a sexual relationship. After they reported their concerns to the administration, they were left on their own to wait in silence for some intervention to take place, interventions that never arrived. No one at the highest level blew the whistle to stop the misconduct.

What this sad story reveals should be a wake-up call for local school staff members, particularly in large urban and suburban high schools like Stamford where anonymity and isolation for both students and staff is common. It's the kind of large school in which both students and staff can get lost and easily fall into problematic behaviors. Stamford High School enrollment was just shy of two thousand students. The core values and beliefs of Stamford High School on the school's website states, "It is our responsibility to make long learning, civic engagement, and respect for tolerance and diversity and for each other."

Yet despite these wonderful values and beliefs, the school's culture allowed a case of sexual misconduct to slip easily into the everyday rhythm of the school and go on even when the misconduct became well known to staff members, the school's administration, the school's social worker, and the district administration (except for the district superintendent). There are important questions that appear unanswered, such as

- Who is Danielle Watkins? What kind of teaching record did she have? Was she involved in other incidents of sexual misconduct? What was her relationship with colleagues, students, parents, and the administration?
- Why was the district superintendent left out of the loop concerning the misconduct? Was it planned so she would not become entangled?
- Why didn't any staff member, guidance counselor, social worker, or administrator approach Ms. Watkins directly and express their concerns and recommend a course of action to help her out of this misconduct? Did they feel it wasn't their job to intervene to help Watkins and that it was someone else's responsibility?
- Why didn't any administrator or staff member report the sexual misconduct to the authorities as mandated by the state?
- Were the school and district administration so overwhelmed implementing school reform and testing programs to make intervening to stop Ms. Watkins's misconduct a priority?
- Why did school politics take precedent in the district's plan to put a stop to the misconduct? Was it the old saw that "it can't happen here in our school" being played out one more time, and "delay, delay" became the district's response?

This is a sad story not only for Ms. Watkins and her teen lover, but also for many members of the professional staff at Stamford High School and in the district office. But the good news, if any, is that it does present an accurate picture of what can happen when sexual misconduct is left to run its own course and those in positions of authority look the other way.

When schools are too busy to care, staff members never get the in-depth kind of training that would put them in the shoes, walk the talk, of Ms. Watkins, her teen lover, Principal Donna Valentine, Assistant Principal Roth Nordin, Assistant Principal Angela Thomas-Graves, Superintendent Winifred Hamilton, Assistant Superintendent Michael Fernandez, District Recourse Director Stephen Falcone, social worker James Cooney, and staff members who were suspicious of Watkins's behavior.

In the meantime, while school reform and increased testing dominate the time and energy of our schools and staff, problems like sexual misconduct continue to rise. As a result, innocent students are in harm's way, as are naïve staff members who have no training in close and intimate contact with students.

Here's an example. A model for training teachers to avoid sexual misconduct is now being carried out for students in teacher training at the University of Delaware.[2] Students studying to become teachers are regularly immersed in training designed to avoid future sexual misconduct with minors, while protecting children under their care. The program places a high emphasis on making appropriate judgments concerning teachers' proper relationships with students. For example, training is designed to make students aware of avoiding situations that may seem harmless but can potentially lead to false accusations, situations like avoiding spending time alone with students in a school setting and not communicating with children outside the realm of education.

The questions raised here are these: How do we get to know our students well and help them navigate through the problems that often come when they enter their pre-teen and teen lives if we demand our teachers avoid one-on-one contact and discuss only "educational" issues? Who owns the "educational" issues, only the school? What about the educational issues complicating students' personal lives? Are they to be pushed aside and banned? Will security be so tight that when students share a concern about personal issues that are getting in the way of their academic success an alarm goes off and the student and teacher are marched off to the principal's office?

Are teachers to be forced to be only academic teachers and avoid any personal contact with students or be models for how adults can serve as trusted advisers and mentors? If leaders in education are promoting the idea of teachers having dual roles as both academic teachers and also as trusted advisers, why the alternate cry to keep teachers away from being positive, caring, helpful role models for students in need of such intervention?

Many teachers came into teaching because they were offered care, support, and encouragement by one or more of their teachers. That's why they are in the classroom. Do we really want to take this gift to help their students with nonacademic problems away from them, warning them to avoid personal one-on-one contact with their students and stick to talking only about educational issues?

Isn't it better to make sure educators are well trained to engage in close contact with their students rather than unilaterally saying, "Close contact is a no-no. It's forbidden. Beware, retreat, hands off." Yes, there are always risks for educators when they choose to serve as advisers for their students, but reinforced by good training the rewards both for students and teachers are well worth the risk.

Let's place the blame for much of sexual misconduct where it rightfully belongs. It's the lack of training that brings educators face to face with the hidden and often emotional issues involved when one enters the personal world of students and a deep trust is formed between teacher and student.

Giving teachers just the data about the number of incidences of sexual misconduct is not enough. Demanding that they avoid one-on-one contact with students and only discuss educational issues is simply a way to scare them and make them pull back from being anything but an academic teacher who simply lectures and avoids any personal contact with students.

We need training that grabs the attention of educators mentally, emotionally, and physically and shakes their defenses so they come to realize that they, like Danielle Watkins, are vulnerable to crossing boundaries and it's time for them to meet their less perfect side and reach out to those whom they can turn to when they find themselves tempted to cross boundaries and become a favorite student's friend, parent, substitute, or even lover.

What is most important to realize is their work as a personal adviser to students is important work and should not be ignored. Students need educators who care for them and educators need students who care for them. This is what education needs to be about, fostering a world of frank discussions and exchanges. That's how students learn to be successful adults and how teachers learn to be successful teachers.

We need to remind ourselves that education is not a safe career if one wants to be a skilled professional. To be good at the job one has to take risks to get better. No pain, no gain, as the saying goes. The process of being a successful educator, whether it is an administrator, counselor, or teacher, goes something like this.

We need to be aware that we come into the profession with our own issues, stereotypes, and problems. We are at best imperfect. We arrive with our own comfort zone for students like us and also an often hidden zone of fear, anger, and revolt toward some students who are different, not like us, and make us anxious. They are students we don't like, even some we are afraid of. And there are students we like too much and feel safe and comfortable with.

To become the competent educator and be free of our background stereotypes we must enter the world of students we care too much for and those we care little about and reconfigure our focus so we learn how to gain easy access with each group. We must learn the hard lesson of not spending too much time with only the students we are attracted to, students who are like we used to be, and avoiding students that balk at our mere presence, create conflict, and disrupt our classes.

We need to learn how to share our attention and care equally and not save it for only the students we value and relate to easily. It's only then that we can call ourselves teachers and put in the necessary work to maintain close relationships with all our students, not just the ones who like us and have similar values and interests. We have to learn how to embrace the others who have a dark side and get to know them well if we are to honorably wear the label of "teacher."

We must remember our schools are for all our children, not just the few who easily win our favor. That's easy work. Building bridges to those who don't buy our stuff is the hard work and that's what makes us certified "teachers," teachers who constantly work toward overcoming biases, stereotypes, and negativity and in place of rejection value students who need our care, help, and sometimes tough love. The goal is to become teachers who are capable of overcoming a self-imposed boundary to "not deal with those kids who are always out to break my balls."

But for administrators and educators to spend quality time with all students and model how best they can become successful students and adults, we need to begin dismantling the current perfect storm in our schools that has sapped the energy of administrators, staff, students, and parents. Creating pathways among every student and staff in the school above all takes time, the will to win, persistence, and the energy and skills to overcome resistance. We can't ask educators to help all their students be all they can be when our schools and staff are being sucked of their energy and commitment to the children.

A perfect storm, a plague, has entered our schools, and it must be dismantled so we can free our educators to be all they can be and do the same for their students. But as the dismantling process goes on, education leaders need to be clear that they need to stop leaving our teachers at risk to sexual misconduct. They need to stop promoting the sham of the value of teachers being advisers and mentors for students to help them resolve their personal and well-being issues but at the same time denying them the quality training the need to do the job right.

Education leaders can't have it both ways. Utilizing the school's public relations outreach to highlight the value of the teachers as advisers and mentors but at the same time sending teachers off unprepared is simply politicking to make the school leadership look good. As a result, teachers like Danielle Watkins get in over their heads, and we see what happened to her.

School leaders at the state, national, and local levels need to reset their priorities and make sure our children and educators come first before the never-ending onslaught of tinkerers trying to make our schools over in their image, not in the image that children and educators know works best. Our students don't need more reforming and testing. They need educators who know them well and can guide them to safe ground and a hopeful future. In the next chapter, I present some concrete ideas that educators can adopt to fast forward the renewal students, parents, children, and educators are calling for.

NOTES

1. Evan Simko-Bednarski, "Assistant Superintendent to Resign in Stamford High Case," *Ctpost*, May 12, 2015, http://www.ctpost.com/local/article-assistant-superintendent-to-resign-in-Stampford-6259674.php.

2. Craig Anderson, "At the University of Delaware Students Are Told Not to Communicate with Children Outside the Realm of Education and School Guidelines." *Delaware.newszap*, January 25, 2015, http://delaware.newszap.com/centraldelaware/137878-70young-abuse-victims-face-continuing-difficulties.

Chapter Nine

A Case Study of What an Administrator Should Do When a Potential Sexual Misconduct Issue Emerges

As discussed in *An Administrator's Guide to Better Teaching Mentoring*,[1] sometimes important issues about setting boundaries occur outside the classroom. Some involve quiet, little-spoken-about relationships between teachers and their students, the kind of issues that "aren't supposed to happen here." These are certainly not simple issues that can be easily addressed, as in the case of relationships that cross over the teacher–student boundary into friendship or even romantic involvement.

Sometimes teachers involved in helping their students work through painful personal experiences take on messiah, savior, friend, or parenting roles, spending more time with certain students, sometimes in evening meetings outside of school. These teachers, some inexperienced in setting boundaries, don't heed the red light of caution and end up crossing over their professional boundaries. Their behavior is often observed by colleagues and administrators who fail to intervene. They can't seem to find the right way to help, the right words of caution, the right skills to bring sense to the situation, and stop the sexual misconduct.

In this vignette, we focus on such a teacher, Shawn Mallory, and his mentor, department chair Randy Edwards. The difference here is that Randy Edwards does try to intervene and advise Shawn Mallory to be careful. He realizes that Shawn is a novice teacher. Shawn may think he knows what teaching is all about, but he has many lessons to learn.

He is well liked by his students, even adored, some might say. As a new teacher, he has brought excitement and zest to his department and the aging school faculty. He's in love with his job, but he may be headed for trouble. Being too involved with needy teens can be risky business, for them and for the teacher. Highly successful careers can easily be detoured when boundaries get blurred. And sometimes the first interventions don't work. Caring colleagues and administrator need to keep trying. Self-awareness and insight sometimes come slowly for those who need help and don't see the danger signs.

With the current rash of school violence, aren't we all looking for teachers who care for at-risk students and can reach out to them? Aren't our schools calling for more teachers to be mentors and advisers, to see that their teaching role should now include helping students solve nonacademic personal problems as well as academic problems? Doesn't helping students resolve personal problems free them to be better academically?

However, before we search out teachers to be mentors and advocates for students, we need to have a support system in place, such as an administrator, mentor, and adviser that can help them give off an early warning sign when a teacher's own personal feelings and needs for relationships spill over into an intimate relationship with a needy teen.

This mentoring relationship involves the health and physical education department chair, Randy Edwards, and first-year teacher Shawn Mallory. Randy followed and found his dream as a physical education teacher and coach. He was a local boy who graduated in the top of his class and starred in three sports—football, basketball, and baseball—deciding early on to be a coach and physical education teacher. He was awarded a scholarship to Springfield College, where he was named All East Coast in both football and basketball.

He returned to the district, where he became an innovative teacher and coach, a new kind of physical education teacher who moved a stale, out-of-touch program into today's world. Randy introduced a number of new programs to address the health and well-being needs of students, such as a weight training room, Project Adventure, peer support for athletes, and workshops on eating disorders and substance abuse problems.

He also developed a wellness program for staff and parents. At least half the staff made use of the training room and participated in faculty workshops to address health and aging issues. When the department chair slot opened up, he was the front runner. He vowed to continue building a model health and physical education program by bringing in teachers who represented new thinking in the field. Shawn Mallory was his first hire. Randy was a natural selection for the mentoring program. His interest and expertise in wellness added an important resource to the team.

Randy also brought an additional resource to the team. He had developed a network with a local university's education department and medical school. He periodically brought in experts to offer a wide range of wellness programs to students, staff, and parents. In turn, he served as an adjunct professor at the university wellness lab. As part of his training, he participated in a workshop on preventing sexual abuse by teachers. It was his first introduction to the topic, one he had never given much thought to.

Sure, he remembered a male teacher he had in high school who had been fired for having a relationship with a senior girl. It was a big story for a few days but eventually faded, with many community leaders saying that it was an aberration; things like that didn't happen in their community. There were rumors sometimes about some teachers getting too involved with a student, mostly a male teacher with a female student, and less often a female teacher with a male student. There were even rumors about same-sex relationships. But they remained rumors.

As Randy immersed himself in his mentoring role, observing his teachers in both their classrooms and coaching roles, he became more aware of how his teachers handled close, personal relationships with their students. He also remembered some of the data and suggestions about teacher–student sexual relationships that he had learned in his workshops.

- There were 110 documented cases of sexual abuse between staff members and students in New York City schools between 1991 and 1995. Most of the cases concerned some kind of willing involvement by smitten students.
- In a 1991 survey of former students at a North Carolina high school, 13 percent of the graduates reported that they engaged in sex with a teacher during their high school years.
- Many teachers lack training and supervision in how to carry on close and intimate relationships with students. If their own personal needs for love and affirmation become thwarted, they may unwittingly seek to meet these needs through a close involvement with a needy student, a student looking for a caring adult, a confidante, whom he or she sees on a regular basis.
- Inexperienced teachers are often more at risk for teacher–student sexual abuse because they don't understand how to create clear boundaries with needy students. Initially flattered by a student's interest and response to their caring, novice teachers may not see the hazards and risks ahead.
- School administrators and colleagues need to recognize the danger signals when they observe them in other teachers' interactions with students, and they need to know how to intervene.
- Teacher–student sexual abuse knows no geographical boundaries; it can happen in any school. It is not just an urban phenomenon.

- Teacher–student sexual abuse is not unlike sexual abuse in other professions. Intimate helping relationships can go awry if the professional involved lets his or her own personal needs take over. Every professional involved in intimate relationships needs ongoing supervision and mentoring.
- Professional training programs and having a professional degree are sometimes insufficient preparation for real-world helping issues.

In mentoring teachers, it is important to observe how they interact with their students on a personal level. Yes, schools want teachers to be involved in helping students who are at risk and lack a significant adult in their lives. Schools need teachers who are responsive and caring and who are positive role models for needy students. But mentors need to be alert when they observe teachers becoming too involved. There are hazards and risks and when mentors observe such behaviors, they need to act.

Sometimes their intervention is rebuffed, but it is still best to take the risk. Turning our backs on problem-creating situations or saying that it's not our job can leave protégés at risk. Like teachers with their students, mentors need to be able to address the nonacademic aspects of their protégés' professional lives and not focus only on the classroom issues. That is an important part of a mentor's work, but not all.

Randy has wrestled with how to address a sensitive issue with Shawn. Shawn is his first hire and in a few short months he has turned into a dynamo, teaching two ninth-grade health classes, two physical education classes, and team teaching a class on tobacco addiction. He has made a quick positive impact. The students, staff, and parents give him high marks.

He is also coaching the girls' volleyball and soccer teams. He seems to be everywhere—eating lunch with students, walking the hallways, greeting kids (he seems to know everyone), and arriving early to supervise the weight training room. He's young and seems to have boundless energy, the kind of teacher every school needs to provide a shot of adrenaline. He's a prize that needs to be cherished, but he should also be taught a lesson about the complex life of a teacher.

Randy understands that Shawn is inexperienced and vulnerable. In spite of his boundless energy and enthusiasm, he makes mistakes, maybe more than other more cautious first-year teachers because he is willing to take on many projects.

The sensitive issue Randy is struggling with is Shawn's seeming overinvolvement with a ninth-grade student named Aileen Lopez. He has noticed that Shawn has been having lunch with Aileen in the school cafeteria on a regular basis. He has also observed Shawn giving Aileen a ride to school on some mornings. Aileen is also on Shawn's soccer team and he seems particularly supportive of her efforts.

On one level, Randy is hesitant to say anything. Maybe all Shawn is doing is trying to help a student who is having troubles. Aileen is new to the district, having moved from an urban school in Philadelphia. Evidently her parents are divorced and she is living with a grandmother. Her younger siblings are living with other relatives in various parts of the country. She is in a new school with little family support. But she seems bright, eager to learn, and is a good athlete.

But the other students haven't welcomed her. She is very attractive and adult-like. It's as if the other students don't know how to react to her. She seems much older than her age of fourteen, as if she belongs in college. Maybe Shawn is just trying to provide a safe place for her until she learns how to fit in.

On another level, Randy has some concerns. Shawn is young, only twenty-four. And the female students think he is, as they say, a hunk. He gets a lot of eyeballing and contact from them. But Shawn, as Randy suggests, is still wet behind the ears, a rookie who has no sense of how to protect himself from crossing boundaries and becoming an item and source of rumor and gossip. While he may be trying to help and support Aileen, he is drawing attention to himself by eating lunch with her on a regular basis and driving her to school.

It may be perfectly innocent behavior, but some of the staff are taking notice and talking. A few have come to Randy and voiced concern, not so much that something is going on between Shawn and Aileen, but that it doesn't look good. It will hurt his chances of getting tenure. Should Randy let things be, hoping Shawn will resolve things himself, or should he speak to the issue and maybe sound a warning and show Shawn how to set some boundaries? Wisely Randy decides he has to talk with Shawn about his involvement with Aileen. Here is the story of their conversation.

Randy: Hey, Shawn. Good to see you? Coffee? Oh sorry, forgot you're a no-caffeine guy. Got some juice, though. Donut? Oh, wrong again. No sugar right? Hey, here's a health bar. I keep them for you health nuts. Seriously, how are the classes and the coaching going? From what I observe, you're really moving and grooving. Kids, staff, and parents all seem to think you're going a great job. And I do too. I haven't heard one criticism. It's very unusual for a young teacher to have such an impact. I guess I know how to hire the right people.

Shawn: Thanks, Mr. Edwards. I mean, Randy. I keep thinking I should call you "sir" or "mister." Yeah, it's been great. The kids and the staff have been great, and so have you. I didn't know what to expect, really. I've been fortunately successful all my life but I wasn't sure how this experience was going to be. My student teaching was in a very conservative school and my mentor there was really out of touch. All he did was turn the classes over to me and go out for a smoke.

But it helped make me independent and rely on myself. I couldn't do some of the things I do here, like Project Adventure, but I survived. The kids there didn't have any of the programs you developed. Looking back I feel like they were being robbed of things that could really help them, like the tobacco workshop. The students here are lucky and I'm just glad to be here. I'm up every morning and ready to go and the day goes by so fast. I can't believe it's February already!

Randy: That's great, Shawn. Your happiness and enthusiasm shows. You've brought a great gift, yourself, to us; to me, the staff, the kids, and the parents. It's much appreciated. I want to do what I can to cherish and support you and your gifts. You have all the makings of a master teacher.

But there is one area I think we need to talk about. It has nothing to do with your teaching performance. You're aces there. And maybe it's not really a problem at all. I just feel we need to get each other's input on the situation and figure out how we should proceed. As your department chair and mentor, I am, after all, responsible for your well-being, learning, and career advancement. I need to address an issue that may get in the way of this process. Does that make sense to you?

Shawn: Sure. I know you're in my corner. I never imagined that you'd be in my classes and at my games so often. I appreciate your interest in me so much. I know you're not out to hurt me. What's going on?

Randy: Again, this may not be a problem, but I've noticed you spending a lot of time with Aileen Lopez. I know she is new and has some personal issues to resolve, and I know she doesn't really fit in with the other students. Ivy Harrison, the school counselor, shared some of that with me. She's counseling Aileen on a regular basis. What concerns me is this. You may be creating the wrong impression by eating lunch with Aileen on a regular basis and giving her rides to school, My take is that you seem to be giving her more attention than what is needed in soccer.

Now, this may not be true, but the wrong impression I'm talking about goes like this. Schools are political places. You're new and you may not grasp that yet. You have no ulterior motives, but some staff members do, and they may draw attention, negative attention, to your seeming over-involvement with Aileen. Rumors can start and rumors can be vicious. Things can be said that may threaten your career, your tenure, even though you're the best new teacher we've had in years.

You have to be sensitive to the picture you're giving other people. Sure, help Aileen, but don't give the impression that somehow there is a friendship, or worse, a romantic relationship, developing between you. That's not fair to you and not fair to her.

Secondly, we are all human. Teachers, in trying to help students, become emotionally involved with them. It's part of the deal. We get to know them, their lives, and their struggles. We feel their pain. Sometimes we want to do more, become their savior, confidante, even take them home so they have a good meal or a decent night's sleep. It's part of being a concerned and caring teacher.

Sometimes our personal desire to help can go too far. I am not saying that this is happening with you and Aileen. But sometimes teachers can become too intimate—become friends or even lovers—with students. It happens. And it can happen to any teacher in this building. That's why some teachers avoid becoming involved in personal relationships with students. They are academic teachers only—they teach their subject and go home.

You know why? Because deep inside they're unsure of themselves, even scared, when it comes to intimate relationships with students. It's safer for them to keep their distance. Their stance is, "Don't tell me about yourself. I don't have to care about you if I don't know your story."

But if you are a caring and concerned teacher, which you are, you have to learn how to set limits and boundaries. We can't be the students' parent or make all the wrongs become right. We can care, listen, give advice, and be there when we can, but we have to draw the line. That's something you're learning, and in a way that situation is a gift because it provides a wake-up call about school life and creating boundaries.

Let me be specific here. I want to hear your response to my query. But here are some specific suggestions regarding Aileen. Stop having lunch with her on a regular basis. Some staff, students, and inevitably parents will pick up on this. Some may start unkind rumors. Don't expose yourself or Aileen to this threat. Stop driving her to school. Again, some people will misread your good intentions and assign less than admirable intentions to you.

Put a stop to the rumors before they start. Support her in soccer, but be aware that you may be giving her too much attention. The other kids and parents aren't dumb; they see it. Don't let it become an issue in your coaching and teaching.

I am not saying end your involvement with Aileen. She clearly wants your support. Withdrawing that isn't useful for her. What I am saying is make the support and the lines clear. Be involved with her in class and in soccer. Be there for her. She will seek you out when she understands that's where the focus of your relationship is. But no phone calls, no rides home. Bluntly, don't be naïve about school life. It can be cruel and hurtful, not just for kids but for teachers as well.

For some teachers, schools are dull places with little novelty and excitement. They live their professional lives on rumors and finger pointing. Learn that lesson. You can be the greatest teacher in the world every day, but if you're drunk at faculty parties or womanizing with a colleague, that's the image that gets talked about. Don't make yourself at risk and vulnerable.

Let me handle the politics. Learn from me how to do it. I'll try to silence any negative references to this situation that may be raised by staff. I don't believe in letting rumors go unanswered. I've learned from experience.

My record as first-year football coach was two and seven and we barely won those two games. I came on board after a championship season, replacing Earl Allen as coach. Allen was a legend here. A lot of rumors started after that season. Getting rid of me seemed a given, but I went to the athletic director and superintendent and made my case. They gave me cover, three years to turn things around.

I'll give you all the cover you need. I'm a local boy and I know how things work. You're in good hands.

Finally, don't worry. This will pass. In fact, as I said, this is a valuable experience for both of us. It's a lesson for you that there's more to learn about school life than teaching. It's good that we're going through this together. I am learning too!

Why don't you think about my observations and suggestions? I've hit you hard, maybe too hard. But I need to say these things if I'm going to be true to my mentoring role and our relationship.

Shawn: Wow. You caught me by surprise with this one. You're right about Aileen. She lives around the corner from my place. Plus she's in my health and PE classes and on the soccer team. I met her at the deli one Saturday morning and we began to talk. She's pretty much alone here. Her grandmother is eighty and quite ill. She has a lot of worries about her family. Her dad went back to Mexico and her mother is living with some guy in Philadelphia who has a drug problem. I guess her mother does too. And her two younger brothers are living in LA with an aunt and her sister is up in Boston with another relative.

She's literally on her own. I guess some of the other students haven't been too kind to her, using racial slurs. It's been tough for her but she's eager to do well and make a place here. So I've tried to spend a lot of my time listening to and guiding her.

No, there's no sexual stuff, just friendship. But I never thought of that until now. It seemed normal, like I was trying to help a kid in trouble. I didn't realize that the spotlight would be on me as a beginning teacher, but I guess it is. Jesus, what do people think? You're right about other things. I find myself spending more time than needed with her at soccer, even giving her a ride home. Whew, never thought about this stuff. As for your suggestions, I think I'd better listen to them. I mean, I wasn't doing anything wrong, but as you say, the picture isn't good. Thanks for noticing.

Perfect ending, who knows? But both Randy and Shawn learned a valuable lesson. Randy gets to affirm his mentoring skills and judgment. He acts, as Shawn suggests, as a guardian angel, warning and protecting this novice from two kinds of threats: threats from the institution that may derail his career and threats that lie within himself that may propel him unwittingly into an intimate relationship, even sexual misconduct, with a needy student.

This kind of relationship can happen in any secondary school to caring but unwitting teachers like Shawn. Intimate one-on-one relationships between caring teachers and needy students can lead to a surrogate parenthood or romantic relationship without intervention from wise, experienced mentors like Randy.

NOTE

1. William L. Fibkins, *An Administrator's Guide to Better Teacher Mentoring* (Lanham, MD: Rowman & Littlefield, 2011), 119–26.

Chapter Ten

Criteria for How the Building Principal Can Build an Effective School Policy to Help Prevent Sexual Misconduct

For policies to be effective in helping prevent sexual misconduct in the schools, they need to be described in public forums and supported by written documents in ways that

1. make sense to school staff so they begin to understand their important roles as observers, confidantes, and helpers.
2. make clear to them in simple terms how they can avoid sexual misconduct and emphasize the notion that every member of the school staff may at some point be vulnerable to sexual misconduct.
3. list sources of support and help in the school and community where they can turn for help if possible misconduct becomes an issue for them.
4. identify colleagues who can help them think through their options and encourage them to seek help.
5. make staff members willing and able to act to intervene when they see a colleague crossing boundaries.
6. stress that every member of the staff has the responsibility to come to the assistance of a colleague headed for misconduct and join with him or her to make contact with the known expert helpers in the school.

The key to any successful policy is demonstrating to each staff member how he or she can serve and be helpful to a colleague before the misconduct becomes out of control and the lives of students and staff members lie in ruin. That is, to serve as their brothers' and sisters' keeper and not leave them alone to pursue a relationship that will probably result in hurt and disgrace for the students involved, their families, and their future.

And to emphasize, helping a colleague and student in danger does not require a doctorate or license in counseling. Caring and courage to intervene do not require letters after one's name. It requires staff members taking notice, observing behavior that is of extreme caring, love, and special or different from other staff–student relations, and making the choice to enter this couple's lives and direct them to help.

This is the tough sell in any policy to help prevent sexual misconduct. Why? Many staff members feel they are not trained to be their brothers' or sisters' keeper. Yes, they feel that's okay with students, but reaching out and helping colleagues with the messy issues involved in sexual misconduct is not a world they want a part of.

They have to be told that that is part of their job, role, and responsibility to act and act quickly, not turn their heads the other way, walk away, and ignore that they see as two people head for deep trouble. Their important role as observer, confidante, and helper is a role that has to be followed up with ongoing training to help staff embrace this new aspect of their role and be ready and set to act when they observe a colleague and student at risk.

This assessment is the heart and soul of any policy on how to help staff and students avoid sexual misconduct. Human contact, face-to-face conversations about what appears to be a developing romantic relationship, and, at times, confrontation are needed to put some reality back into the lives of two people lost in sexual misconduct that has little chance of continuing.

This is not to say that the more legalistic aspects of a sexual misconduct policy are not important, but they lack the power of healing that face-to-face contact, confrontation, offers. Here are some examples that usually dominate the content of many schools' sexual misconduct policies, policies that usually omit the powerful helping role of colleagues and instead rely on legalistic tactics. Yes, legalistic tactics are important but lack a human dimension, carried out by a small group of administrators and support staff far from the world of everyday school life and focused on sexual misconduct as a "wrongdoing" rather than a risky act of human need to find care and belonging in a lonely school world.

1. Screen new and current employees with background checks that include fingerprinting.
2. Centralize record keeping and designate one case coordinator to whom all rumors, allegations, or complaints are channeled.
3. Educate employees and students about expectations for behavior, the responsibility to report suspected wrongdoing, and the proper channels for doing so.

4. Staff needs to pay attention to rumors, whispers, and complaints from students and bring them to authorities to investigate and determine their merit.
5. Inform students, parents, and school employees where to file formal and informal complaints.
6. The policy and problems of sexual misconduct should be discussed in all school assemblies, orientation with new staff, and meetings with parents.
7. School personnel should be trained to look for suspicious behavior and required to report suspected sexual misconduct.
8. Reporting, grievance, and investigation procedures must be followed up immediately.

These are examples of the legalistic side of sexual misconduct, which in most schools rule the way sexual misconduct is handled. Descriptions such as "wrongdoing, investigation, screen employees, background checks, case coordinator to whom all rumors, whispers, allegations, and complaints are channeled, report suspected wrongdoing, formal and informal complaints" make up the substance of most school policies.

These policies that suggest that need for a surveillance system to create an impenetrable wall preventing predators from crossing the school border and leading vulnerable and naïve students into sexual misconduct. It's a system that operates secretly outside the regular school organization and is given unbridled power to investigate and charge staff members who appear to be involved in sexual misconduct. It's a system that is built, thrives, and survives on gathering rumors and whispers and in which any staff member can become a target and can be found guilty in the court of public opinion.

However, these legal maneuvers only serve to keep a few predators away and do nothing to train staff on how to handle close and intimate relationships with needy students and how to intervene when they observe a colleague crossing boundaries and heading for sexual misconduct.

Educating staff that their main concern and responsibility is to report suspected wrongdoing is simply treating them as cops on patrol and does little to help them to be prepared to avoid sexual misconduct and be a source of support for colleagues.

The hard work for building principals is being able to develop a vision of how best to make sure sexual misconduct training and interventions are simply not left to developing a surveillance system to keep predators out. That's an easy path to follow. Appoint a case coordinator to gather rumors, whispers, complaints, do fingerprinting and background checks, teach students, parents, and staff how to report so-called wrongdoings, and you are in business.

But it's a business that only touches the surface of the sexual misconduct problem. Staff members are still left untrained and ill-prepared to avoid sexual misconduct. The policy has been written with legalistic overtones and threats, but victims of sexual misconduct, both staff and students, are usually too enraptured to be threatened by legalistic warnings.

Finding caring and a seemingly safe place to belong tends to blind needy educators and students from the risk they are taking and the dangers involved in crossing boundaries.

Policies are important as a starter, but they are no match for ongoing training for staff that has the goal of convincing them that they are all vulnerable to sexual misconduct given the events in their personal and professional lives. The predators may be stopped from crossing the school border, but the staff members and students within the school can also be at risk even though the word on the street is "it can't happen here."

Yes it can, and it takes more than policies to protect our students and staff. It takes a well-trained staff ready to act as supportive colleagues, not law enforcement members on the lookout for wrongdoing.

Conclusion

The major message in this second edition is that sexual misconduct between needy students and educators is not going away. Our large secondary schools, many enrolling over two thousand students, are highly sexualized places. These are schools that also encourage anonymity, isolation, and loneliness, a scenario that encourages sexual misconduct for needy students and educators looking for a caring relationship.

However, the good news is that schools can do a much better job of observing the beginning of sexual misconduct and intervening to stop the liaison before the lives of both the students and educators lie in ruin. But many schools have had their resources and commitment to intervene diminished because their helping and caring mission has been given a lower priority by the powerful forces of the reform movement.

The reform movement has captured the energy, will, and commitment of educators to protect and care for all their students, especially the ones that may be at risk of sexual misconduct, and transformed their top mission and priority to implementing reforms designed by reformers who know little about how local schools work, their needs, and the ideas for change local staff view as important.

As a result, when cases of sexual misconduct arise in the schools and recommendations are made, such as calling for more supervision of educators by administrators, training for staff, educators on the frontlines of the school being encouraged to intervene when they observe a colleague crossing boundaries, and establishing easily accessible support groups educators and students can turn to when they become involved in close and intimate contact such as school athletics, clubs, and so on, they are usually met with a positive reaction by school leaders.

But often that positive reaction by school administrators dies an early death. The reality is that given the pressures of reform for time and resources, there is little time and money available for training on how to supervise, observe, intervene, and be sources of support for at-risk students and staff.

Reforms are a powerful, well-funded bulldozer that rolls into town and uses its will, powerful media, and political connections to get its way. The pleas by knowledgeable parents and citizens for more protection and care for their at-risk children often go unheard. Their voices get lost in the manufactured good news in today's media-driven culture, which is all about good news numbers such as high test scores, college acceptances, Ivy League colleges entered, scholarships earned, and athletic victories and awards. The cries of students in trouble with sexual misconduct are hushed up, yet still a secret everyone seems to know about.

However, as building administrators understand, schools can't have it both ways. They can't commit their total resources and staff to implementing all the aspects required by reformers and still have resources, staff time, and commitment to mount a successful intervention network. Choices have to made: reformers control budgets versus budgets for staff training and support for interventions to help at-risk students.

A network that includes increased staff supervision, training of staff and students, and a variety of support and counseling interventions must be implemented so there are a number of open doors for students and educators to find help and be guided away from wrecking their lives and careers.

But there is growing evidence that the tide is beginning to turn against reform efforts, while only a few years ago reform was the only game in town and schools were forced to get on the bandwagon, no questions asked. For example, as in New York,[1] Governor Andrew Cuomo earlier this year pushed through legislation that calls for student test scores to count 50 percent of a teacher's evaluation, up from the current 20 percent.

The New York State teachers unions were incensed, believing that test scores are a simplistic and unfair means of assessing teachers. So were many parents, who joined a boycott movement that resulted in an estimated 165,000 students opting out of the 2015 standardized tests. A recent study says standardized testing is overwhelming the nation's public schools.[2]

The number of standardized tests U.S. public school students take has exploded in the past decade, with more schools requiring too many tests of dubious value, according to the first comprehensive survey of the nation's largest school districts.

A typical student takes 112 mandated standardized tests between prekindergarten classes and twelfth grade, a new Council of the Great City Schools study found. By contrast, most countries that outperform the United States on international exams test students three times during their school careers.

The heaviest testing load falls on the nation's eighth graders, who spend an average of 25.3 hours during the school year taking standardized tests, uniform exams required of all students in a particular grade or course of study. Testing affects even the youngest students, with the average pre-K class giving 4.1 standardized tests, the report found.

The study analyzed tests given in sixty-six urban districts in the 2014–2015 school year. It did not count quizzes or tests created by classroom teachers and it did not address the amount of time schools devote to test preparation.

It portrays a chock-a-block jumble in which tests have been layered upon tests under mandates from Congress, the U.S. Department of Education, and state and local governments, many of which, the study argues, have questionable value to teachers and students. Testing companies that aggressively market new exams also share the blame, the study said.

"Everyone is culpable here," said Michael Casserly, executive director of the Council for the Great City Schools. "You've got multiple actors requiring, urging and encouraging a variety of tests for very different reasons that don't necessarily add up to a clear picture of how our kids are doing. The result is an assessment system that is not very effective."

In one of the most notable attempts to reduce testing, Miami-Dade superintendent Alberto Carvalho earlier this year cut the number of district-created end-of-course exams from 300 to 10 and eliminated them entirely for elementary schools.

"I believe in accountability," said Carvalho, who runs the country's fourth-largest school district. "But fewer assessments of higher quality are better. . . . What we have now across the country is confusing, hard to navigate and, I believe, abusive of both teacher and student time."

But even testing supporters agree about an overload. "For those of us who support annual assessments, it doesn't mean we support this craziness," said Kati Haycock, president of the Education Trust, an advocacy group focused on reducing the achievement gap. "There's a clear problem here."

For example, in 40 percent of districts surveyed, test results aren't available until the following school year, making them useless for teachers who want to use results to help guide their work in the classroom, Casserly said.

Jeffrey Cipriani teaches second grade at Orchard Gardens K–8 Pilot School in Boston. Even though his students are not in a grade that is required by federal law to be tested, the Boston Public Schools has him administer reading tests to his students three times a year. Because the tests are individual and can be as long as ninety minutes, it takes Cipriani about three weeks to test the whole class.

"It's a colossal amount of time," he said. "I probably spend about 60 hours not teaching reading but just sort of giving those assessments. They are valuable but not that valuable."

"We can't assess our way to academic excellence," said Carvalho, of the Miami-Dade school system.

And financial woes continue to plague Common Core rollout.[3] Five years into the biggest transformation of U.S. public education in recent history, Common Core is far from common. Though forty-five states initially adopted the shared academic standards in English and math, seven have since repealed or amended them. Among the remaining thirty-eight, big disparities remain in what and how students are taught, the materials and technology they use, the preparation of teachers, and the tests that are given. A dozen more states are considering revising or abandoning Common Core.

One reason is that Common Core became a hyper-charged political issue, with grassroots movements pressing elected leaders to back off. Some conservatives saw the shared standards as a federal intrusion into state matters, in part because the Obama administration provided grant funding. Some liberals and conservatives decried what they saw as excessive testing and convoluted teaching materials. The standards are a hot topic in the Republican presidential race. Last month, Barack Obama recommended limiting the amount of class time students spend on testing, saying excessive testing "takes the joy out of teaching and learning."

But politics isn't the only reason for the turmoil. Many school districts discovered they didn't have enough money to do all they needed to do. Some also found that meeting deadlines to implement the standards was nearly impossible.

The total cost of implementing Common Core is difficult to determine because the country's education spending is fragmented among thousands of districts. The *Wall Street Journal* looked at spending by states and large school districts and found that more than $7 billion had been spent or committed in connection with the new standards. To come up with that number, the *Wall Street Journal* examined contracts, e-mail, and other data provided under public records request by nearly seventy state education departments and school districts.

The analysis didn't account for what would have been spent anyway—even without Common Core—on testing, instructional materials, technology, and training. Education officials say, however, that the new standards required more training and teaching materials than they would otherwise have needed, and the Common Core prompted them to speed up computer purchases and network upgrades.

Much more money would be needed to implement Common Core consistently. Some teachers haven't been trained, and some schools lack resources to buy materials. Some states haven't met the goal of offering the tests to students online, instead of on paper with No. 2 pencils.

For some urban districts struggling to pay for basic educational needs, preparing for the standards has been challenging. The Philadelphia school district unveiled a plan in 2010 to implement Common Core and won a $500,000 grant from the Gates Foundation. But a budget crisis the next year resulted in nearly four thousand layoffs, including of some of the individuals putting the plan in place.

"It was something of a perfect storm, where expectations were rising while resources were diminishing," says Christopher Shaffer, Philadelphia's deputy chief of curriculum, instruction, and assessment. "Grant money was spent on summer training that wasn't well attended. The teachers were all on vacation," says Ann Brown, then a district curriculum official.

Ms. Brown says district leaders sent the new standards to school principals without sufficient guidance. Teachers were struggling with the new standards when she arrived at the George W. Nebinger Elementary School as principal and began to train them.

Since then, the district has created a teacher's guide for integrating the standards into lesson plans. Administrators conduct weekly training sessions. But budget problems have meant that little has been spent on buying new instructional materials, officials say.

Preparing teachers to implement the standards can be costly. New Mexico spent $5.2 million training about 11,600 educators—about half of the state's total, officials say. Some states turned to grants from the $4.3 billion federal educational reform program called Race to the Top to help fund a move to the standards. But now most of that money is spent, leaving school districts to shoulder the continuing costs.

In the end, schools can't protect and help care for at-risk students and staff in the present school environment with its overemphasis on reform, the lack of time, resources, and commitment for increase supervision of staff, ongoing training for staff, revised counseling intervention programs headed by a full-time personal counselor, and support to assist busy building principals in carrying out their mission to know and watch closely over all students.

But that doesn't give school leaders license to give up and accept reform as a never-ending perfect storm and plague. Rather, the hope of this book is that if reform has resulted in lowering the commitment, spirit, energy, and care level of school staff, it has also helped them to reflect upon how things could be better for students, parents, educators, and administrators.

Hopefully this book will give them some ideas and programs to consider. Sexual misconduct is a prime example of the kind of problem that has the power to ruin the lives of students and educators. Sexual misconduct isn't composed of just one problem, but rather a series of unresolved developmental problems coming together in a perfect storm to set a student and educator off on a course of no return unless someone throws them a life jacket.

We need more caring educators who are not hesitant to throw a life jacket before it's too late. It's not difficult to notice a student or staff member needing help if we as educators know them well and are tuned in to sense their cry for help even if it is mixed with a defiant "leave me alone, not your business, go save someone else" wall of resistance.

Knowing our students and colleagues well and being a person they can trust helps a lot to reduce their resistance. But then again it takes supervision and practice to know how to throw a life jacket accurately so it arrives on target and those in trouble can grasp it and be willing to be pulled back to shore when life will demand some answers.

Finally, for far too long educators have focused their entire attention on predators to help stop the growing problem of sexual misconduct in the schools and left the vast majority of teachers untrained and vulnerable to the same problem they blame solely on predators.

This is similar behavior to a family spending all their time preaching to their children to stay away from other kids who they see as troubled but doing nothing to help teach them how to navigate through the difficult issues that children face as they grow older. As a result, they enter teenage life without the necessary skills needed to handle the chaotic life they find in secondary schools.

Parents who focus all their energy on building walls to keep troubled peers away but neglect training their children to face the reality of the world they are entering are like education leaders who follow the same patter—keeping the bad guys, the predators, outside the school gate but doing the minimal to make sure their staff is not at risk to the same misconduct.

Yes, identifying and excluding predators is important, but it is only a small part of the problem and the work that must be done. Focusing all our energy on building walls and securing the borders of the school to keep predators out is a strategy that misses the major source of sexual misconduct in our schools: needy teachers, coaches, and students.

It's time for school leaders to redirect more of their recourses to train their staff to help them avoid falling into the dark hole of sexual misconduct.

NOTES

1. Joe Nocera, "How to Grade a Teacher," *The New York Times*, June 16, 2015, http://www.nytimes.come/2016/06/16/opinion/joe-nocera-how-to-grade-a-teacher.html?action=Homepage&module=opinion-c-left-regio.

2. Lyndsey Layton, "Study Says Standardizes Testing Is Overwhelming Nation's Public Schools," *Washington Post*, October 24, 2015, http://www.washingtonpost.com/local/education/study.

3. Michael Rothfeld, "Financial Woes Plague Common Core Rollout," *Wall Street Journal*, November 2, 2015, http://www.wsj.com/articles/financial-woes-plauge-commmon-core-rollout-144651250.

References

Adams, Jane Meredith. "Schools Failing to Protect Students from Sexual Abuse by School Personnel, Federal Report Says." *Edsource*, February 8, 2014. http://edsource.org/2014/schools-failing-to-preport-students-from-sexual-abuse-by-school-personnel-federal-report-says/57023#.VUEghyFVikp.
Anderson, Craig. "At the University of Delaware Students Are Told Not to Communicate with Children Outside the Realm of Education and School Guidelines." *Delaware.newszap*, January 25, 2015. http://delaware.newszap.com/centraldelaware/137878-70young-abuse-victims-face-continueing-difficulties.
Archibold, Randall C. "A Chill at Stuyvesant High." *New York Times*, September 21, 1999, 1, 8 (B).
Associated Press. "Evidence against Teacher Barred." *Boston*, October 13, 1994. http://nl.newsbank.com/nl-search/we/Archives?p_action=print.
———. "Maine Teen-ager Testifies of Sex with Ex-teacher." *Boston Globe*, March 9, 1995, 26.
———. "Maine Third-Grade Teacher Acquitted of Sexually Abusing Two Teen-Age Boys." *Boston Globe*, March 11, 1995, 14 (Metro).
Boyle, Maureen. "Detective Lyons Investigated Shockro Case 'Relentlessly.'" *South Coast Today*, January 8, 1998. http://www.s-t.com/daily/01-98/01-98/a01o003.htm.
Boyle, Maureen, and Bridgette Sweeney. "From Trust to Betrayal and Lingering Pain." *South Coast Today*, December 31, 1997. http://southcoasttoday.com/daily/12-97/12-31-97/a01o005.htm.
Briggs, Bill. "Coach's Harsh Style Brings Success, But Some Wonder If It's Worth It." *Denver Post*, October 12, 2003. http://www.denverpost.com/cda/print/?.1674.36%7E76%7E1690925.html.
———. "Lopez: Hoopsters Not about Money." *Denver Post*, October 12, 2003. http://www.denverpost.com/Stories/0.1413,36%7E76%7E1692617.00.html.
———. "Success a Constant among Lopez's Teams." *Denver Post*, October 12, 2003. http://www.denverpost.com/cda/article/print/0.1674.36%7E76%7E169074.00.html.
Buettner, Russ. "Teacher, Teen on the Run for Love." *Newsday*, May 11, 1995, 6 (A).
Carnegie Council on Adolescent Development: Task Force on Education of Young Adolescents. *Turning Points: Preparing American Youth for the 21st Century*. Washington, DC: Carnegie Council on Adolescent Development, 1989.
ChucksConnection Film Review. "Mr. Holland's Opus." http://www.chucksconnection.com/holland.html.
Colorado Hoopsters. *News & Announcements*. January–February 2005. http://coloradohoopsters.com.

Demoretcky, Tom. "Teacher Cleared of Fondling." *Newsday*, January 26, 2000, 29 (A).
DenverChannel.com. "Girls' Basketball Coach May Face 100 Counts Related to Sexual Assaults." August 20, 2004. http://www.thedenverchannel.com/print/3669544/detail/html.
Education Week. "Preventing Sexual Misconduct." March 10, 2004. http://www.edweek.org/ew/ewstory.cfm?slug=26B1,h23&keywords=sexual%2ab.
Estrella, John. "10 Days of Allegations, Questions, and Headlines." *South Coast Today*, February 23, 1997. http://www.southcoasttoday.com/daily/02-97/02-23-97/a011o005.htm.
Farkas, Steve, and Jean Johnson. "Kids These Days: What Americans Really Think about the Next Generation." *Public Agenda* (1999): 8–9, 11, 13, 16–19, 25–26.
Feller, Ben. "Sexual Misconduct in Schools Tabulated." Associated Press, July 1, 2004. http://info.mgnetwork.com/printhispage.cgi?url=http%3A//www.tampatrib.com?news?M.
Fibkins, William L. *An Administrator's Guide to Better Teacher Mentoring.* Lanham, MD: Scarecrow Press, 2002.
———. *An Educator's Guide to Understanding the Personal Side of Their Students' Lives.* Lanham, MD: Scarecrow Press, 2003.
———. *Preventing Teacher Sexual Misconduct.* Bloomington, IN: Phi Delta Kappa Foundation, 1996.
———. *Students in Trouble: Schools Can Help before Failure.* Lanham, MD: Scarecrow Press, 2005.
Fillo, Mary Ellen. "Shadows Stalked Girls' Glory Days." Associated Press, March 10, 2002, 5–7 (A1).
Fine Line Features Synopsis. "Carried Away." http://www.finelinefeatures.com/carried/synopsis.htm.
Finn, Robin. "Growth in Women's Sports Stirs Harassment Issues." *New York Times*, March 7, 1999, 1 (A), 24 (L).
Gabbard, G. O., J. D. Bloom, C. C. Nadelson, and M. T. Norman, eds. *Psychodynamic Approaches to Physicians' Sexual Misconduct.* Washington, DC: American Psychiatric Press, 1991.
Goldberg, Carey. "Manhattan Teacher Surrenders in Kidnapping of Teen-age Girl." *New York Times*, May 17, 1995, 1 (A), 4 (B).
———. "Nationwide Hunt for Teacher and Girl, 15." *New York Times*, May 11, 1995, 1, 8 (B).
Hartford Courant editorial. "End Mr. McKernan's Career." *Hartford Courant*, June 4, 2004, 10 (A).
Hendrie, Caroline. "Abuse by Women Raises Its Own Set of Problems." *Education Week*, December 2, 1998. http://www.edweek.org/ew/vol-18/14women.h18.
———. "Cost Is High When Schools Ignore Abuse." *Education Week*, December 9, 1998. http://www.edweek.org/ew/vol-18/15handle.h18.
———. "Experts Convene on Sexual Abuse by Teachers." *Education Week*, April 9, 2003. http://www.edweek.org/ew/ewstory.cfm?slug=30abuse.h22.
———. "In Youth's Tender Emotions Abusers Find Easy Pickings." *Education Week*, December 2, 1998. http://www.edweek.org/ew/vol-18/14tactic.h18.
———. "Preventing Sexual Misconduct." *Education Week*, March 10, 2004. http://www.edweek.org/ewstory.cfm?slug=26Abuse-B1.h23&keywords=sexual%20ab.
———. "Report Examining Sexual Misconduct Taps Some Nerves." *Education Week*, July 14, 2004. http://www.edweeek.org/ew/ew_printstory.cfm.?slug+42Abuse.h23.
———. "Sex with Students: When Employees Cross the Line." *Education Week*, December 2, 1998. http://www.edweek.org/ew/vol-18/14abuse.18.
———. "Sexual Abuse by Educators Is Scrutinized." *Education Week*, March 10, 2004. http://www.edweek.org/ew/ewstory.cfm?slug=26Abuse.h23.
Herbert, Bob. "An Ugly School Situation." *New York Times*, May 17, 1995, 19 (A).
Irvine, Martha. "Colleges Offer Classes on Relationships." Yahoo!News, February 13, 2005. http://www.yahoo.com/news?tmpl=story&cid=514&u=ap/20050213/ap_On_re_us/teaching.
Jackson, Anthony W., and Gayle A. Davis. *Turning Points 2000: Educating Adolescents in the 21st Century.* New York: Teachers College Press, 2000.

Jacobs, Andrew. "School Official Charged with Molesting Students." *New York Times*, May 22, 1999, 3 (B).
Kane, Arthur, Adam Thompson, and Bill Briggs. "Coach in Sex Case Apparent Suicide." *Denver Post*, December 12, 2004. http://www.denverpost.com/cda/article/print/0.1674.36%7E53%7E262282.00.html.
Kaufman, Susan. "When Teachers Mix Socially with Students." *News & Observer*, September 29, 1994, 1, 12 (A).
Kreytak, Steven. "Gym Teacher Charged with Rape." *Newsday*, March 8, 2000, 8 (A).
Kreytak, Steven, and Gregg Sarra. "'Connection' Broken." *Newsday*, November 11, 1999, 5, 60 (A).
Lam, Chau. "No Jail for Coach in Affair." *Newsday*, March 21, 2000, 29 (A).
Layton, Lyndsey. "Study Says Standardized Testing Is Overwhelming Nation's Public Schools." *Washington Post*, October 24, 2015.
Levinson, Michael. "Ex-Principal Rejects Naming Honor." *Boston*, December 12, 2004. http://boston.com/news/local/articles/2004/12/ex_principal_rejects_naming_hon.
Mattson, Rick. "Mr. Holland's Opus." http://ransomfellowship.org/M_MrHolland.html.
Mohan, Geoffrey. "Guilty in Teen Sex." *Newsday*, February 22, 1997, 27 (A).
Moy, Kimberly W., and William Schubert. "Coaches Avoid Charges in Sex Allegations." *Hartford Courant*, January 10, 2002, 7 (A1).
Murphy, Shelley. "Teacher in Abuse Suit Defends Actions." *Boston*, September 14, 2004. http://www.boston.com/news/local/articles/2004/09/14/teacher_in_abuse_suit_defends_act.
National Association of Secondary School Principals (NASSP). *Breaking Ranks: Changing an American Institution*. Reston, VA: National Association of Secondary Principals, 1996.
———. *Executive Summary of Breaking Ranks II: Strategies for Leading High School Reform*. Reston, VA: National Association of Secondary School Principals, 2004.
Nocera, Joe. "How to Grade a Teacher." *The New York Times*, June 16, 2015. http://www.nytimes.com/2015/06/16/opinion/joe-nocera-how-to-grade-a-teacher.html?action=Homepage&module=opinionc-col-left-regio.
Noguera, Pedro. "Special Topics: Transforming High Schools." *Education Leadership*, May 2004. http://www.ascd.org/publications/ed_lead/200405/noguera.html.
O'Brien, Ellen. "Police Press Questions to School in Rape Case." *Boston Sunday Globe*, February 16, 1997, 4 (B).
O'Hagan, Maureen, and Christine Willmsen. "Misconduct Often Goes Unpunished by Districts." *Seattle Times*, December 15, 2003. http://seattletimes.nwsource.com/news/local/coaches/news/daytwo.html.
———. "What School Districts Can Do." *Seattle Times*, December 15, 2003. http://seattletimes.nwsource.com/news/local/coaches/news/school.html.
Ontario Province Ministry of the Attorney General. "Chapter I: The Nature and Scope of the Review." Review of Kenneth DeLuca Case, 1999. http://attorneygeneral.jus.gov.on.ca/english/about/pubs/robins/ch1.asp.
———. "Chapter III: Extent and Nature of Teacher–Student Sexual Misconduct." Review of Kenneth DeLuca Case, 1999. http://attorneygeneral.jus.gov.on.ca/english/about/pubs/robins/ch.3.asp.
Quintanilla, Blanca Monica. "Track Coach Faces Molestation Charges." *Newsday*, July 22, 1998, 29 (A).
Rhode, David. "Probation for Teacher Guilty of Abuse at Stuyvesant." *New York Times*, August 19, 1999, 1 (B).
Rothfeld, Michael. "Financial Woes Plague Common Core Rollout." *Wall Street Journal*, November 2, 2015.
Salcedo, Michele. "Teacher in Rape Case Popular in School." *Newsday*, February 22, 1995, 7 (A).
Sheehan, Peter. "Safety for All Is Goal of Background Screening, Training." *Long Island Catholic*, October 20, 2004, 1, 3.
Simko-Bednardski, Evan. "Assistant Superintendent to Resign in Stamford High Case." *Ctpost*, May 12, 2015. http://www.ctpost.com/local/article-Assistant-superintendent-to-resign-in-Stamford-6259674.php.

Simmons, Roberta G., and Dale A. Blyth. *Moving Into Adolescence: The Impact of Puberty Changes and School Context.* New York: Aldine De Gruyter, 1987.

Slade, Margot. "Yes, Statutory Rape Is Still a Rather Big Deal." *New York Times*, June 11, 1995, 9 (E).

Smith, Estelle Lander. "Jail for Teacher in Student's Sex Abuse." *Newsday*, July 19, 1994, 4 (A).

———. "Teen to Testify at Teacher Sex Trial." *Newsday*, May 6, 1994, 25 (A).

Sorrentino, Mary Ann. "John Shockro Not the Only Guilty Party in Sordid Case." *South Coast Today*, January 7, 1998. http://www.s-t.com/daily/01-07-98/c04op105.htm.

Southington Journal. "Town's Disgust Outlasts a Statute of Limitations." *New York Times*, January 14, 2002, 17 (A).

Stover, Del. "What Happens When a Teacher Accused of Harassment Is Innocent?" *National School Boards Association*, May 16, 2000. http://www.nsba.org/site/print.asp?TRACKID=&VID=58&ACTION=PRINT&CID=332&.

Strauss, Valerie. "Why Teachers Are Fleeing Arizona in Droves." *Washington Post*, June 19, 2015. http://www.washingtonpost.com/blog/answer-sheet/wp/2015/06/19.

Swiggart, William, Karen Starr, Reid Finlayson, and Anderson Spickard. "Sexual Boundaries and Physicians: Overview and Educational Approach to the Problem." Vanderbilt University Center for Professional Health, 2001, http://www.mc.vanderbilt.edu/root/vumc.php?site=cph&doc=742.

Theisen, Sylvester P. "Interfaith Sexual Trauma Institute (ISTI) Book Review of John C. Gonsiorek, ed., *Breach of Trust, Sexual Exploration by Health Career Professionals and Clergy.*" April 22, 1996, http://www.csbsju.edu/isti/Book%20Reviews/gonsiorek.html.

Thompson, Adam. "Summer Tourneys Where It's at for College Hopefuls." *Denver Post*, October 12, 2003. http://www.denverpost.com/Stories/0.1413.36%7E76%1690740.00.html.

Thompson, Adam, and Bill Briggs. "Cult of Personality." *Denver Post*, October 12, 2003. http://www.denverpost.com/cda/article/print.0.1674.36%7E76%7E1692763.00.html.

———. "Sex Charges Shadow Girls' Coach." *Denver Post*, October 12, 2003. http://www.denverpost.com/cda/article/print/0.1674.36%7E76%7E1693470.00.html.

Tieffer, Leonore. "On the Therapist's Couch." *Newsday*, January 5, 1997, 37 (C).

Vaishnav, Anand. "Top Official Targets Abuse by Educators: Driscoll to Urge Vigilance." *Boston*, August 24, 2004. http://www.boston.com/news/local/articles/2004/08/24/top_official_targets_abuse_by_ed.

Willmsen, Christine, and Maureen O'Hagan. "Coaches Continue Working for Schools and Private Teams after Being Caught for Sexual Misconduct." *Seattle Times*, December 14, 2000. http://seattletimes.nwsource.com/news/local/coaches/news/dayone.html.

———. "Misconduct Registry, More Training Needed for Washington Coaches." *Seattle Times*, December 16, 2003. http://seattletimes.nwsource.com.news.local/coaches/news/state.html.

Wishnietsky, Dan. "Reported and Underreported Teacher–Student Sexual Harassment." *Journal of Education Research* 3 (1991): 164–69.

Wyatt, Edward. "Schools Show Jump in Reports of Sex Abuse." *New York Times*, May 23, 2001, 1, 7 (B).

Yaffe, Elaine. "Expensive, Illegal, and Wrong: Sexual Harassment in Our Schools." *Phi Delta Kappa* (special report, November 1995): 37.

Yan, Ellen, and Robin Topping. "School Sex Abuse: Sachem H.S. Teacher Held in Case Involving Teen." *Newsday*, June 25, 1993, 3 (A).

Zehr, Mary Ann. "Report Tallies Alleged Sexual Abuse by Priests." *Education Week*, March 10, 2004. http://www.edweek.org/ew/ew_printstory.cfm?slug=26Catholic.h23.

www.ingramcontent.com/pod-product-compliance
Lightning Source LLC
Chambersburg PA
CBHW031553300426
44111CB00006BA/293